What! No Tom Peters endorsement?

Did it ever occur to you that, if Tom Peters really read all the books he endorsed, he would never have enough time left to write his own? Here's a few honest, from the heart, comments from real people like you who have read this book. I personally guarantee you'll enjoy, and be challenged by its contents. I even guarantee it will make you live longer. If it doesn't, I will be gladly refund your money, and your time.

I laughed, I cried, it became a part of me! Well, actually, I lied about the crying part. Throughout this book, I found Lindsay's wit enjoyable and to the point. He had me smiling and, sometimes, laughing out loud. I saw parts of corporate America on almost every page (but never my company!?!?!?). I'm already using some of the ideas, so it really did become a part of me!
Dave Gunby, EDS

I was asked to review a video and book of Lindsay's for an upcoming speaking event. As I read excerpts from the book, I started to share them with other marketing managers and, from there, the book had a life of its own. For three days I chased it as it made frequent appearances in many offices with the telltale phrase, "Did you read this? This, us, them, or we use to …..!"
Carl Morrison, Burndy Electrical, Manchester, NH

I love your book. Please send me three more copies as soon as possible.
Lynn Fink, MS Ed., Henderson, NC

Focused on challenging the way we think both "about" and "inside" our organizations, Lindsay has a unique and successful way of sharing his extensive experience and knowledge about transforming organizations.
Dr. Robert Ruotolo, Allied Signal Aerospace,
Phoenix, AZ

This was a very different and fresh approach to TQM. What a great analogy, that by whacking the problem you are only compounding it and it will come back stronger. We distributed your books to our whole facilitator team and they were very well received.
Sortia Averill, SmithKline Beecham, Philadelphia, PA

The Whack-A-Mole Theory is one of the most enjoyable books I've read on creativity and innovation. Lindsay knows what he's talking about and presents it in a fun, readable, and practical manner. He presents a very honest and thorough look at problems in organizations and how one goes about solving them. I loved this book and consider it a valuable tool for implementing organizational change. This is a must read for anyone who is interested in increasing their general level of creativity and innovation.

Susan Linscott, General Mills, Minneapolis, MN

The Whack-A-Mole Theory has a powerful message that must be heard by Japanese organizations.

Noburou Hayashi, Future Vision Institute of Japan

This book is fun! Lindsay's unique writing style, combined with his insights and ideas, capture the essence of creativity. It's a must read!

Jim Lang, Parkridge Hospital. Rochester, NY

In the Whack-A-Mole Theory Lindsay Collier takes a scythe to the weed patch of classical organizational thinking. He can take you where you've always dreamed of going and, what's more, the journey will be fun.

Don Cassidy, Merchants Bank, Aurora, IL

Your books are the most requested reference materials from the students in my creativity and innovation classes.

Roger Syverson, Professional Value Services, Minneaplois, MN

The Whack-A-Mole Theory is a creatively written book on creativity. It is fun to read and loaded with simple ideas for expanding thought process.

Tom Kyser, Xerox Corporation, Rochester, NY and author of *Mining Group Gold* and *Team Power*

The value of a reference book is in direct portion to the number of *dog ears*, post-its, and highlighted sections the reader has marked. My copy of Lindsay's book is full of notes, highlights, and colored pieces of paper on ideas and concepts that I need to remember. He has insights on every page and his book is a valuable resource to us.

Barry MacMillian, Central Maine Medical Center, Lewiston, ME

Lindsay's writing is straight forward and sometimes shocking. This book hits the reader over the head and makes you ask the question, "Why are we still doing this?". It is a book which will give you new creative energy and change the way you do your job.

Gail Bober, St. John Fisher College, Rochester, NY

If you are totally satisfied with the way things are, don't let your employees read this book.

Dave Schantz, Organizational Change Consultant

The
Whack-A-Mole Theory

Creating Breakthrough And Transformation
In Organizations

Lindsay Collier

Additional copies may be obtained from

WhAM Books
PO Box 352 • West Henrietta, NY 14586
Tel 716-334-4779 Fax 716-334-4779

Dedication

This book is dedicated to my wife, Jan, and my children, Stephen, Gregory, and Laurel. They have been my inspiration through the years. And to my daughter-in-law, Lisa, who always makes me feel good. I love you all.

Special thanks to my editor, David R. Young.

Table of Contents

About the Author

Lindsay Collier has spent more than a quarter of a century developing ways to enhance the creative capacity of people at work. Recently he has led dozens of workshops and spoken to thousands of people from all kinds of organizations on how to create breakthrough and transformation. His unique integration of material from various disciplines results in effective approaches which create real change.

Lindsay spent most of his years at Eastman Kodak Company where he developed techniques, trained corporate staff members, and provided consulting to enhance creativity, innovation, and strategic exploration processes within the company. He formed his own consulting firm in 1991 so he could bring this breakthrough material to other organizations. A popular speaker and workshop leader, he prides himself in being able to practice what he preaches—being different and thinking differently. Lindsay strongly believes that humor is a major resource in the workplace (he even designed and built a humor room at Kodak), so his work tends to be spiced with a somewhat weird sense of humor which makes it even more fascinating.

Lindsay has been President of the Western New York Futurists chapter of the World Future Society, President of the Rochester (New York) Professional Consultants Network, and Chapter President and District Director of the Institute of Industrial Engineers. He is a colleague of the Creative Education Foundation in Buffalo, and a member of the Innovation Network, the National Speakers Association, the

Organizational Development Network, the World Future Society and the American Society for Training and Development. He lives with his wife, Jan, in the town of West Henrietta, a few miles south of Rochester, New York. Creative Edge Associates offers a wide array of products and services focusing on creating breakthrough in organizations. If you would like to know more about these or are interested in having Lindsay speak to your group or organization, please contact him at:

Creative Edge Associates
PO Box 352
West Henrietta, NY 14586

Telephone 716-334-4779
Fax 716-359-9744
E-Mail LindsayCollier@msn.com

INTRODUCTION

If you are tired of reading about Total Quality Management (TQM), reengineering, empowerment, teams and team nets, learning organizations, benchmarking or any of the other many fads promising to cure the ills of business and are interested in some new thinking that may really create some breakthrough in the future, read on. Hector Berlioz once said, "Time is a great teacher. But, unfortunately, it kills all its pupils." Is there a lesson here for the leaders of our organizations?

The past 5 to 10 years have brought a tremendous influx of "ultimate solutions" to organizational problems, most of which have resulted in no change—or change in the wrong direction. For example, the majority of TQM programs have been very disappointing overall and, if you ask the right people, have even blocked positive change and eroded morale. Many reengineering programs have created terribly negative morale and resulted in little change. Very few learning organizations are really learning anything. This book does not propose a new program. It suggests how to change organizational thinking. TQM, learning organizations, reengineering and many of the other popular programs of the day can be of value only if there is a shift in the thinking of organizations. I hope the contents of this book will give you some great ideas for making these shifts.

The ideas expressed here have not been pulled out of a hat but are the result of many years of careful observation and countless "gut level" discussions by people at all levels and in all types of organizations. You may think I'm talking about your organization but the truth of the matter is that the dynamics are pretty much the same in all types of organizations.

This book is intended to "ruffle some feathers" because there are a lot of feathers out there in business that need some ruffling. I may slay a few of your "sacred cows" but it's been said that, "sacred cows make the best hamburgers." I want you to think very differently about the dynamics of your organization, and how these dynamics impact your ability to create exciting futures. And I want you to think about how these dynamics might change to allow you to create some real transformation, breakthrough, and futures you never thought possible. This book breaks an existing paradigm that suggests change must be a painful experience. People tend to move away from pain, not toward it. The explorations, ideas, and processes discussed in this book are designed to bring some *fun* into the change process. If, by the time you finish this book, you haven't questioned dozens of your assumptions about your organization and made some drastic shifts in the way you think about creating very different, more powerful, futures, then I haven't done the job I've set out to do. And if you don't find yourself enjoying the experience of making these thinking shifts then I'll be very disappointed. Let me tell you a story.

Once upon a time two companies, one American, one Japanese decided to have a boat race along a local river. Both teams practiced hard and long and, on the big day, the Japanese won by a mile. The American team was very discouraged by the loss, and morale sagged. Corporate management decided that the reason for the crushing defeat had to be found. A "Continuous Improvement TQM Team" was set up to investigate the problem and to recommend corrective action. The problem was that the Japanese team had eight people rowing and one person steering whereby the American team had one person rowing and eight people steering. The American Corporate Steering Committee hired a consulting firm to do a study of the management structure. After some

2

time and millions of dollars, the consulting firm concluded that: "Too many people were steering and not enough rowing."

To prevent losing to the Japanese again, the team's management structure was totally reorganized to four steering managers, three area steering managers, one staff steering manager, and a new performance management system for the person rowing the boat (to give more incentive to work harder). "We must give him empowerment and enrichment. That ought to do it." The following year, the Japanese won by two miles.

Humiliated, the American Corporation laid off the rower for poor performance, sold all the paddles, canceled capital investments for new equipment, halted development of a new canoe, gave a "high performance award" to the consulting firm, and distributed the money saved as bonuses to the senior executives.

Sound familiar? In my experience, breakthrough change in organizations hardly ever results from programs with labels like TQM, teaming, performance management, continuous improvement, reengineering or any of the other many programs that pass through organizations like oat bran. Although there may be a few isolated instances of success, most of these programs provide no shifts in thinking that will move an organization toward real breakthrough. Breakthrough change results from transformation, which begins with transforming the collective thinking of organizations. To change the thinking, it is necessary to think about thinking, something we rarely take the time to do. The managers of companies engaging in the latest program to save their companies—those who believe real change is already taking place—should talk at a "gut" level with their employees to learn what *they* see happening. Of course, this is difficult for most managers because there are rarely enough open and trusting relationships to allow these conversations to take place.

Let's take a look at a few observations that affect an organization's ability to create transformation and breakthrough. Most of these will be discussed in more detail in later chapters.

Observation #1

Most organizations spend their energy solving problems and never create anything. Like ducks, they are great at paddling but a little shaky at flying. Moving from problem solving to creating is a major theme of this book.

Observation #2

Solving problems is like hanging wallpaper or pushing a cork into the water. If you have ever tackled wallpaper then you know that the job consists of getting the paper in the right position and then spending most of the time chasing air bubbles around. When you push an air bubble down it comes up somewhere else and when you suppress a problem in an organization it also usually comes up somewhere else. And, like the cork in water, the harder you push on your problems, the harder they want to push back. I believe we are continually underestimating the importance of the system's relationship to the dynamics in organizations. Typical downsizing programs introduce some tremendously destructive forces within organizations which, in the end, may program these organizations for future failure.

Observation #3

Most organizations are navigated through rear-view mirrors. There is a very strong attachment to the past that drives many companies. I know of no major firms that have a process for scouting the future. Those who claim to have such a process probably have a strategic program for projecting their current future forward. This is quite different from creating a future based on the pull of a strong vision of what is possible.

Observation #4

Many organizations spend the bulk of their energy whining and moaning rather than really changing anything. People love to complain about the weather (which they can't change) and their workplaces (which they can change). If we could only channel the energy spent whining and moaning to productive change processes we'd enable these organizations to create breakthrough.

Observation #5

Some people, like race horses, wear blinders and can only see things that are directly in front of them. There is a huge portion of possibilities available to organizations that is out of their fields of view. How to find these possibilities is another major theme of this book.

Observation #6

People, in general, are too comfortable in their work. It's like owning a Ferrari and driving it only in schools zones. The inventors of the Nautilus system found that muscle developed only when it was brought almost to the point of tearing. I believe brains and organizations are similar in this regard. Breakthrough never comes from the comfort zone and, since many organizations spend most of their time being comfortable, they will not achieve very exciting futures.

Observation #7

Managers love cute words and short-term solutions to their problems. A company's reception area will often display missions, visions, principles and a variety of other similar nicely framed documents. Read the buzzwords and then ask a few people (those who look like they may have some connection with actually putting product out the door) what those words really mean. The answers may surprise you. I have seen companies that listed "breakthrough thinking" as one of their guidelines only to find out that there wasn't a person to be found who had the slightest idea what it meant. There are managers who can't complete a sentence without using the word *paradigm,* yet they have had terminal cases of "paradigm paralysis" for years.

Observation #8

Restructuring is almost always the solution but is hardly ever the problem. I sometimes call this the "Bird Cage Theory." Think of an organization as a cage full of birds sitting on their perches. Every now and then someone gives the cage a good shaking so that the birds fly around. When the shaking stops, they all land on new perches. The metaphor clearly describes most companies' restructuring processes, and their results.

Observation #9

Truth rarely moves up in an organization. Each level acts as a shield for truth and, the more levels, the higher the probability that the top person never sees the real world.

I hope the ideas and thoughts in this book will allow you to stretch your thinking and encourage you to ask some provocative questions regarding your own situations. I have used many of these ideas in team-building sessions and workshops and hope that many of you will be able to do the same. I urge you to be as creative as you can while using the ideas in this book to stimulate dialogue around change in your own organization. And remember, creating transformation doesn't have to be painful. Why not have fun while doing it?

In the first chapter I'll define the Whack-A-Mole Theory and show how this influences the ability of organizations to produce creative thinking about the future. Chapter 2 will describe what breakthrough is, and isn't, and Chapter 3 will look at a few of the illusions that tend to block organizations from real breakthrough and transformation. Chapter 4 contains some fascinating material about organizational paradigms along with questions that will help take you beyond these paradigms. In Chapter 5 we'll have some fun and look at metaphors that will clarify thinking within organizations and, in Chapter 6 we'll dig up a few more "sacred cows." Chapters 7 and 8 will take a new look at creativity in the workplace and the role of humor as a resource. We'll look at the role of dialogue in Chapter 9 and then, in Chapter 10, focus on a process that will help you move your own organization closer to breakthrough and transformation. Provocative questions are included throughout the book and at the ends of most chapters. These are questions I ask frequently in my workshops and presentations and I invite you to create your own organizational dialogue around them. They are stimulating, fun, and powerful and have the potential to begin shifting the way people think about what is possible. And that's how breakthrough starts.

Chapter 1

Hi Ho, Hi Ho
We're Off to Whack
Some Moles

"If we think more about failing at what we are doing than about doing it, we will not succeed."—*Warren Bennis*

Getting The "T" Out Of Can'T

How often do you hear the word "can" in your organization? My guess is that you hear "can't" much more often. Organizations tend to be very good at magnifying negative feelings and reactions and very weak at magnifying the positive. They are often much better at "cant's" than they are at "cans." A lot of energy is spent whining and, although whining may have some therapeutic value for the whiner, its real value is to release you to go on to better things. I've used "whine and jeez" parties in some organizations to temporarily mourn the passing of the way things used to be. But you must eventually focus on what you want to create in the future if you really hope to create change.

I am not quite sure why "can't" spreads through an organization easier than "can." I do know, however, that this needs to be reversed. Real change can't occur while everyone is privately or publicly saying, "I can't." It is certainly not as simple as *The Little Engine That Could*, but a good starting point is to provide leadership that helps people feel that they can do anything they put their minds to.

The Whack-A-Mole Theory

I have long been fond of reading Peter Drucker's books. Somewhere in one of his earlier books I remember his saying that problem solving gets you nowhere. This raised my sensitivity to just how much people at work engage in solving problems and how little they focus on creating anything new.

Even the use of creativity in business is generally applied to problem solving rather than to creating something. I was observing a high level group in action when I was reminded of a time in my childhood. As a teenager, billions and billions of years ago, I looked forward to the annual fair in our town. My favorite game was the Whack-A-Mole game. For those of you who have not been blessed with the opportunity to play this game, let me explain. The game is played by waiting for a "mole" to poke its head out of one of several holes in a table-like game board. When one pops up, you whack it with a large soft-rubber mallet. Then another mole will emerge which you must whack as quickly as possible. The game continues from there and it is a great deal of fun. For some strange reason it makes you feel good. I was never quite sure of its purpose and I also never remember winning anything. Elmer Fudd had this problem with "wasketty wabbitts." Just for the fun of it lets take a look at what is happening in the Whack-A-Mole game:

1. When you whack a mole (a person, a thing, a problem), another pops up somewhere. This would seem to suggest that there is a system at work.

2. When you are finished, you are tired and happy but you haven't created anything new.

3. Its a lot of fun though and, since you have been fulfilled, you think you have accomplished something or changed some behaviors. The feeling of accomplishment comes from whacking a LOT of moles not from the importance of the moles you whacked. How many of you have set up long lists of "small" to-do goals so you could cross off more of them? As a friend once said to me, "That's why pin ball machines have scores in the millions rather than the tens or twenties."

4. If they were real moles, they would be very mad. Problems that have been bashed and are mad can come back to haunt you in many ways.

After observing this behavior in hundreds of groups, I find that there isn't much difference between the behaviors exhibited in organizations and the Whack-A-Mole (WhAM for short) game. We whack moles (solve problems), have a lot of fun, and never win anything of value. While whacking moles we believe that we are really accomplishing something important. But when we're finished, we're back to where we started and our pockets are emptier. Robert Fritz, in his thought provoking book, *The Path of Least Resistance*, calls this the "reactive-responsive" orientation. (See Appendix 1 for book references.) He suggests it sets you up for endless vacillation between non-compatible solutions to problems. For example, a reaction to today's problem might suggest that you centralize. But the closer you approach centralization the stronger will be the forces that urge you de-centralize.

Peter Senge gives some wonderful examples of this in his book, *The Fifth Discipline,* along with diagrams of the archetypes that define this dynamic. The trouble with the WhAM orientation is that it deals mainly with the past. When you are busy dealing with the past it is difficult to do a good job creating an exciting future for your company. For example, when you are dealing with improving "old plans" you can only end up with improved "old plans." Solving the problems of today only gets you back to today. If you are interested in creating an improved future for your organization you'll need to anticipate the future, create something new, and be driven by the gap between your vision of this future creation and the reality of today.

Another problem is that we often whack the wrong moles. Electric cars were suggested as the solution to the energy crisis years ago and now as the solution to environmental problems. But if every gasoline powered car were replaced tomorrow with an electric car, the need for charging capabilities would create a new energy crisis. And the disposal of all their used batteries would create another environmental headache. Electric cars will not solve the energy problem nor the environmental problem. They will merely substitute different problems. One mole down, another pops up. If we look at what we want to create, getting people's minds and bodies connected to their work and play, we may invent creative ways to solve the transportation-energy-environmental problem that do not have a negative effect on the environment. The other orientation that Fritz mentions in his book is the "creative orientation." The major difference is that you are defining something you intend to create. When current reality is defined, the energy for creating breakthrough comes from the creative tension between what you want to create and the current reality.

The word "vision" has been very popular (and badly misused) over the past few years. I have seen groups carry out "visioning" exercises which are often just that—exercises. Visions are created with most of the energy focused on getting the words right. Then they are filed away until, months later someone says, "Hey, what was that vision statement we developed?" It has been said that, "For every vision, there is an equal and opposite revision" which suggests that the staying power of the common, rather wimpy, visions is not too good.

"So what?" you ask. I believe there is a major lesson here that could enable organizations to shift to a mindset for creating breakthrough. Just imagine what would be possible if some major American businesses (auto manufacturers might be an interesting starting point) stopped whacking moles and began focusing their energies on creating a wonderful product. And you certainly don't need to be a major-league organization to make that same shift in your thinking. Creating something new is fundamentally quite different from eliminating problems. We all need to get in the creative orientation. The problems will take care of themselves as we begin to close the gap between what we want to create and current reality.

This Ship is Going Down, Throw Away the Life Boats

A lot is said these days about the fact that American business is driven by reaction to short-term news. Management reaction to a downturn is quite predictable and also very often wrong. When things don't seem to be going well, there is a tendency to get rid of the very things that may be able to help. As someone once said, "I'd give my right arm to be ambidextrous." When the prevalent orientation is reactive and responsive (which most are) you might expect reactions designed to satisfy the immediate pain. Like a non-swimmer who suddenly finds himself in the water, the tendency is to panic and begin paddling like mad. You know what the results of this often are.

So, when we have a bad quarter, we cut costs by cutting out the people and functions that may be the most able to help create new breakthroughs that can achieve greatness in the future. This reaction always sets up a chain reaction of feelings and events because organizations are clearly complex systems. When we push down on one thing, something else pops up. (Sounds like the Whack-A-Mole game doesn't it?) These feelings and events can often create a downward spiral that makes recovery difficult. Cost-cutting measures create unhappy, depressed people who have lost self confidence and confidence in their employer. They begin setting up protective behavior, stop all risk taking, talk negatively about their jobs, point fingers at all the "others" who are at fault, etc. This can set up a terribly complex series of dynamics, all of which detract from achieving a great future for the organization.

I've been reading about the recent decision by the US. Postal Service to again raise the postal rates. They say that the reason for the increase is that more money is needed because mail volume is down. You would think that even the Postal Service might be able to deduce that mail volume has a tendency to go down when the rates go up. Raising the rates more will drop the volume more and, eventually, something will come along to replace the Postal Service altogether (if it already hasn't). Poor decisions like this are common in business. Maybe it's time to enter the age of "opposite" decision making—take every management decision and do just the opposite. Another rather predictable reaction is reorganization. Many companies have gone through so many reorganizations in the past few years that they now call it restructuring to make it a little less embarrassing. I find it interesting that we so often change the names of worn out programs to make them sound new.

We trained hard, but it seemed that every time we were beginning to form into teams, we would be reorganized. I was to learn later in life that we tend to meet any new situation by reorganizing: what a wonderful method it can be for creating the illusion of progress while producing confusion, inefficiency, and demoralization.

This sounds like a contemporary statement but, it was said by the philosopher Petronius in 60 AD! We are still creating the illusion of progress by reacting to short-term downturns by reorganizing, even if we now call it restructuring. It seems we are very slow learners as well. Reorganizing might be advantageous in growth situations and occasionally during ma-

16

jor downsizings (which we now call "rightsizing"). But this reaction also sets up some complex dynamics, most of which are protective rather than productive. I have seen situations where people would react according to what "this week's reorganization plan" was. It's difficult to accomplish anything worthwhile when people are preoccupied with questions such as:

Who do I work for this week?

What is currently safe and unsafe?

Is my job in jeopardy?

What is the program of the month?

What are the right buzz words today?

Am I working myself out of a job?

Because of the reactive-responsive orientation of most reorganizations, their resulting structures tend to be cyclical. When you are centralized, the movement will be toward decentralization. When you are decentralized, the movement will be, you guessed it, toward centralization. This is the nature of reactive-responsive behavior. It's kind of like being in a rocking chair where you just rock back and forth, feel really good about it, but never go anywhere. As the great Alfred E. Newman once said, "Just because everything is changed doesn't mean anything is different."

Reorganizing is not the only reaction organizations have up their sleeves. Benchmarking is another very popular "in thing" lately. This is defined as finding other companies in your business who are not as good as you so you can say, "See, we aren't that bad." We often initiate new "programs" which provide tighter measures of our business activities. But creating more measurement tasks bogs more people down in meaningless, non-value-adding work and raises their need to protect themselves by making the figures come out right.

There is also a strong drive to find things easy to measure which rarely are true measures of effectiveness.

Then there are programs aimed at motivating people at work. We create the illusion of empowerment of employees (sometimes renamed *associates*). This is often done with performance management programs that treat people like pigeons by providing forced feedback to them when they do a good job at something that is easy to measure but probably has little to do with business effectiveness.

Real, lasting, and profound change will not occur in organizations through programs that are reactive or responsive in nature. As Robert Fritz suggests, "The path of least resistance will most often take you back to where you are." You can't change the course of a river without changing the river bed. Similarly, you can't make profound changes to enable breakthroughs in organizations by simply overlaying programs onto the existing culture. You need to make some shifts in the "cultural bed" of the organization. It may not be easy, but it may be the only choice you have.

It has been said that bureaucracy is the art of making the possible impossible. In 1978, the Chancellor of the University of London reported four items of verbal statistics. Draw from them what lesson you will. The Lord's Prayer has 56 words. The Ten Commandments have 297 words. The American Declaration of Independence has 300 words. The directive of the European Economic Community (EEC) on the import of caramel and caramel products has 26,911 words.

I define breakthrough as the art of making the impossible possible. To work toward this, let's take a look at how your organization stacks up in the game of Whack-A-Mole. Take a few minutes to answer these questions. Don't just play with them. Take a hard look at them. Be honest. It may be uncomfortable to take a real stretch on some of these, especially if you are doing it in the company of some associates who may be the very people who created the conditions. Remember, real change doesn't take place unless you get outside of your box. It also helps to take others out there with you. Once you begin discovering the potential out there, you'll be amazed at what you've been missing and what you can accomplish.

Thought Provokers On Mole Whacking

1. How many moles have you whacked today? What, specifically, were these moles? For each one, to what extent did whacking it bring you closer to your vision?

2. Describe some typical moles that your organization spends a lot of time whacking.

3. If you weren't spending your time whacking moles, what would you do to add more value to your business?

4. What is it that you or your organization *should* be creating?

5. How might you go about creating this instead of whacking moles?

Chapter 2

The Nature of
Breakthrough
in Organizations

"An optimist sees an opportunity in every calamity; a pessimist sees a calamity in every opportunity."—anonymous

What is Breakthrough?

It is important to understand what breakthrough really means because the word has a tendency to be misunderstood. It also has a tendency toward "buzzworditis," a deadly disease which has been fatal to some very valuable words (the word "paradigm" is currently suffering from this). The disease begins when an interesting word is planted in the minds of business people who use it without understanding its meaning. Remember when "brainstorming" meant "having a group of people generate ideas without evaluating them"? Today, "brainstorming" means, "Let's bring up a few ideas that we can bash to smithereens so we can say we were creative."

If businesses and organizations are to achieve highly successful futures they must be able to concentrate on three areas:

- The achievement of excellence
- Becoming innovative
- Scouting the future and its implications

Out of necessity, most American companies are totally immersed in the pursuit of excellence. You simply can't survive without quality. The problem with this is that, since everyone is doing it, it is a matter of survival. Becoming excellent at what you do today does not necessarily buy you a great future, it just keeps you in the game for a while. And while you are concentrating on being excellent at what you now do, there is a likelihood that you are ignoring some real possibilities that just may be the driving forces of your company's future. There is some need for breakthrough in finding new ways to achieve excellence but breakthrough is mainly concerned with creating innovation and scouting the future. *Breakthrough involves creating a new pattern, or paradigm, rather than improving on a new one.* Improving the old is perfective change. Creating breakthrough is transformative change. There is a transformation to a new state. As George Land suggests in *Grow or Die*, all organizations go through a formative, normative, and integrative stage. Practically everything goes through a grow or die process in which initial formation and slow growth is followed by a period of hearty growth followed by a leveling off (Figure 2.1).

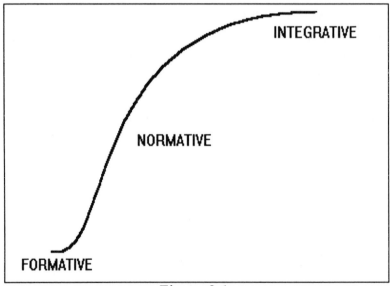

INTEGRATIVE

NORMATIVE

FORMATIVE

Figure 2.1

Breakthrough in organizations follows these stages: formative, normative, and integrative. The formative stage is one of coming into being—a time during which the organization searches for identity and pattern. The task is to invent a pattern that works. There is good news and bad news in this situation. On one hand you have worry, anxiety, and confusion. On the other you have energy, excitement, hope, and promise. The sky's the limit and it is all driven by a high level of energy. At this stage in a growth cycle:

- Mistakes are acceptable—and perhaps not even considered as mistakes. When a child is learning to walk, do you get upset when he falls?
- Innovation is not only valued, it is mandatory.
- Market focus is high and you are out there feeling the pulse of your customer.
- Goals are clear.

There is usually a smooth transition from formative to normative and it is usually done in a climate of positive growth. In the normative stage there is steady growth and fine tuning of the system. The pattern is developed and working. There is good and bad news here as well. The good news is that there is profit and comfort—the bad news is that work may not be as enjoyable and exciting as it used to be. For some it is positive, predictable, comfortable, and profitable, and it provides a sense of accomplishment and success. For others it is negative, boring, political, regimented, and business as usual. At this stage,

- Mistakes tend to be frowned upon and not viewed as learning opportunities.
- Innovation is given "lip service" approval but is subtly punished.
- Market focus is no longer high.
- The goal becomes: "Let's stay on this curve forever."

These are classic late normative responses:

• Get back to basics.

Work smarter, not harder.

Reorganize, cut costs, downsize.

Refuse to acknowledge that the system is not working.

Hope for an upswing.

• Do nothing—maybe it will get better on its own.

• Redefine the business and get back to the basic activities of early normative.

The best time for breakthrough is in the last third of the normative phase. Unfortunately, most organizations will wait until the integrative stage where the need and the pain are the greatest.

In the integrative stage, redefinition occurs and a new direction is taken. This redefinition is different from that between the formative and normative stages because it is expansive, not reductive. This transition period is either "rough" or "less rough"—it is never comfortable. The main reason is because it is growing out of an entrenched culture and this creates problems:

False starts - Procedures, policies, organizations and strategies from phase 2 mentally get in the way and keep anything new from growing.

Chronic uncertainty - Comfortable people have to develop a greater tolerance for ambiguity and uncertainty. The rules change from "taking orders" to "taking initiative."

Organ rejection - The organization works to "kill" the new system and, since the old system tends to be very strong, this is fairly easy to do. People cling to the thought, "If it ain't broke don't fix it."

Transition as an event - People don't perceive a problem until an event makes them aware of it. The "boiled frog" analogy is often used to explain this. If a frog is put into a pot of boiling water it will jump out to safety. If the same frog is put into a pot of water at normal temperature that is slowly heated to boiling, it will stay there and boil to death.

Overnight job shifts - Some very competent people may become incompetent overnight by being shifted into positions they cannot handle, or do not yet understand. Breakthrough creates a new curve of growth as shown in Figure 2.2. This new growth is not just more of the same, it's a paradigm shift. The rules change, the thinking changes, and the organization prepares to go on to new growth.

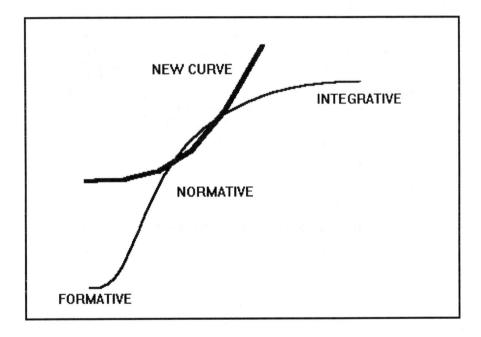

Figure 2.2

Breakthrough extends the boundaries of possibility in both process and results. It actually creates new potential.

As shown in Figure 2.3, something is created that does not now exist (except in the minds of people). It is interesting to note that breakthrough does exist in people's minds right now. The question is, "Why leave it there?" George Land in his book, *Breakpoint and Beyond,* notes that we are all carrying the future around with us in our heads right now. For the most part, we are blinded to the breakthrough potential shown in Figure 2.3. Most of today's efforts are aimed at creating perfection by moving from current performance up to the potential we now see. This perfective change is certainly necessary but real breakthrough is transformative and carries us into potential we didn't even know we had.

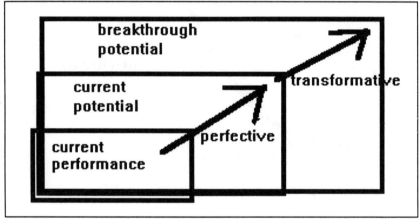

Figure 2.3

We are often misled into thinking that we are involved in breakthrough when, in reality, we are well within the area of our current potential. It takes some real work and some stretching to create transformative, or breakthrough, change. This type of change rarely comes from total quality management programs. In fact, I have seen many examples where TQM has actually created some strong blockage for future breakthrough. Many organizations are so hung up on the details of their quality programs that they are locking out possibilities for breakthrough. Small, creative companies, if they are smart, aim their competitive efforts at large companies that are bogged down in their quality programs. They may be easy targets because they have their heads buried too deep in the "quality sand."

Breakthrough lets go of the past rather than building on it.

Letting go of the past is one of our biggest challenges. Since many of us are driven by our obsession with the past and our desire to build on to it, being pulled by our vision of the future doesn't always sit well.

Why is Breakthrough So Elusive?

We tend to be trapped in our "boxes." There is rarely much incentive to venture outside these boxes because it may be dangerous out there. We are used to being safe and rather like it that way. As a matter of fact, there is a certain "OKness" about non-achievement in work. In many organizations people can make a very good living spending their entire career focusing on staying out of trouble. Not achieving particularly good results, along with a good excuse is often adequate. We sometimes have our excuses lined up early for the failure we are programming ourselves to achieve. Large organizations are designed to protect what they have rather than to seek something they don't have—something new. As the number of successful products in an organization increase, so are the forces of protection strengthened—and the likelihood of innovation weakened. Nearly all breakthrough products come from outside the giant companies normally associated with the product. They often come from people who were once in large companies and, because of the bureaucracy, couldn't get their ideas listened to. There are some wonderful breakthrough product ideas just waiting in the cobwebs of large companies. Will they ever break loose?

Another major breakthrough block lies in our inability to be good listeners and our strong tendency to engage in poorly focused conversation. It was once said that "No great idea ever entered the mind through the mouth." Making assertive statements about what we *will* achieve in the future has a powerful effect on helping us realize these achievements. What potential was set into motion when Kennedy said, "We will have a man on the moon by 1970"? But we rarely make these statements—it's more comfortable to be wishy washy. If we are going to achieve breakthrough, we must learn how to conduct productive conversation. Conversation aimed at possibilities will help us create the visions we need for success. Conversations of opportunity will create the bridge between possibilities and action. And, when it is time for action, the conversations need to concentrate on what needs to be done and how to overcome any breakdown in the way of its accomplishment.

The Future Exists Right Now

We have grown to believe that the future is something that other people invent for us. We just react to it or dance with it when it comes to us. Here is an interesting thought for you: Where are the next breakthrough ideas right now? Our normal belief is that they don't exist yet. If you look at it another way, it makes sense that they exist somewhere in the minds of people. They just haven't appeared yet—whatever is necessary just hasn't lined up. If the future exists in some minds right now, the question is, "How can we get it out sooner?" This suggests some very high potential in effective processes for scouting the future. Unfortunately, many companies are much more interested in reacting to the past and present.

There is gold waiting for those who care to ask the right questions and carry out the right processes for getting at the futures we are carrying with us today.

The Keys to Achieving
Breakthrough in Organizations

Later, in Chapter 10, we will take an intense look at a process to help achieve breakthrough. It involves the creation of excitement, the shifting of thought paradigms, the creation of strong visions and the establishment of a "Go For It" attitude. But first, let's take a look at some other interesting and slightly irreverent observations about organizational life.

Thought Provokers Concerning Breakthrough

1. What percentage of the energy in your organization is consumed in processes engaged in achieving excellence, innovation and scouting the future?

2. Where is your organization on the growth curve? What does this suggest to you?

3. If you could extend the boundaries of possibility, what would be some opportunities that might avail themselves to you?

4. What are some things you need to let go of?

5. What are some things that keep you inside your "box"?

6. What do the conversations in your organization tend to focus on?

Chapter 3

The Illusions of Management

"The things that got you to where you are today are not the things that will get you to the future."—Peter Drucker

The Illusion of Commitment

For years we have been trying to learn how we might be able to gain true commitment of people to those things needed to create real breakthrough. More often, we seemed to be putting people into situations in which they felt they had to say yes when asked about their commitment because it was easier than explaining why they were not committed. True commitment comes from a fairly complex set of relationships between alignment with a vision, personal values, and the dynamics of workplace relationships.

In *The Fifth Discipline*, Peter Senge identifies seven levels of commitment, only one of which he actually calls commitment:

- **Commitment** Wants it. Will make it happen. Creates whatever is needed to make it happen.
- **Enrollment** Wants it. Will do whatever can be done within the "spirit of the law."
- **Genuine compliance** Sees the benefits of the vision. Does everything expected and more. Follows the letter of the law. A good soldier.
- **Formal compliance** On the whole, sees the benefits of the vision. Does what's expected and no more. Pretty good soldier.
- **Grudging compliance** Does not see the benefits of the vision. But also does not want to lose job. Does enough of what's expected because he has to, but lets you know he is really not on board.

- **Noncompliance** Doesn't see the benefits and won't do what's expected.
- **Apathy** Neither for nor against. No interest. No energy.

I have rarely seen a situation where there is true commitment or enrollment. Most situations, whether you want to admit it or not, are controlled by some form of compliance. This is a particularly nasty and elusive problem since this lack of commitment usually doesn't surface until failure occurs. People will rarely admit their lack of commitment and managers assume everyone is committed because they are not complaining.

The Illusion of Empowerment

The word "empowerment" is very popular today. When a word is popular it can spell real disaster since many people feel that simply saying the word can substitute for the real thing. If someone tells you they have an empowered work group, don't necessarily believe them. Twenty-five years ago Douglas McGregor from MIT coined the terms, Theory X and Theory Y. What he was saying then still makes sense after all these years but has, unfortunately, been terribly misunderstood. He said that management tends to have either Theory X or Y assumptions about people. Theory X means they assume people are motivated by either a carrot or a stick and Theory Y that they are motivated intrinsically by the work itself.

Quite obviously, truly empowering people at work cannot be done by managers that are using Theory X assumptions. While most would say they are definitely Theory Y, the large majority are really Theory X. So when there is talk in companies about the empowering of people, they are only words. When there are problems, like a bad quarter in sales, the reactive behavior will never be consistent with truly empowering people. I think, given a choice between no empowerment and the illusion of empowerment, people are much better off with none. At least they are relatively sure where they stand. When blacks came north, they said there was as much discrimination in the north as in the south, but the north concealed it. You never knew where you stood. They said that in some ways it was more comfortable in the south because you knew where you stood.

Structural Answers to Non-Structural Problems

Most problems or concerns seem to be answered with structural solutions. If there is a bad financial quarter, it is followed by discussions of downsizing or reorganizing. Cut the staff, stop training, decentralize, centralize, etc., etc. If there is a drop in innovative productivity we must need an office of innovation. If sales are dropping we must make some shifts in our sales functions. There always seems to be a way to turn business problems into opportunities to change structure.

The majority of business concerns emerge from internal problems which result in a failure to use the capacity of associates and not from having the right boxes with the right people in them. One large company that spent a great deal on research and development found it was getting little in the way of innovative products. Someone decided that there should be a new unit developed which would be an *office of innovation*. We can't get people to be innovative in their workplace so let's set up a place where they can take their ideas. The real problem is how to create an environment that stimulates creativity and innovation *within* the existing framework. But it is easier to develop a new unit than it is to influence the culture of a company. The creation of a new unit just adds to the problem because of the complexity it adds to the organization.

In the past several years many companies have undergone repeated restructuring efforts and, with each one, have tended to be worse off. Each restructuring takes its toll in eroding the confidence of people and steals energy from the real work that needs to be done. Every time there is an organizational change, relationships and responsibilities must be redefined and this can be a very difficult task indeed.

Surfing the Big Trends

I am not a surfer. Lake Ontario is just not a Mecca for surfing. But, if I understand it correctly, surfing involves getting out beyond the waves and watching carefully for a big one to come along. When you spot the right one, you catch it and ride it for all it's worth. There seem to be some similarities here with organizational life. Many organizations contain lots of people who are just waiting for the right wave and just as many who are up riding the current ones. These waves never quite get you to the beach. When one dwindles you must go look for another. The idea is to find the biggest wave you can so you can get the longest ride.

The "quality" wave is the biggest one at the present time and there are a lot of surfers on it. When this one hits shore the beach is going to be full and there will be a lot of people out looking for a new wave. Over the years, there have been countless "trend waves" most of which have fallen harmlessly on the beach. Some of them, however, have done some damage to the beach. Think of it as eroding the beachhead. There are even a few that actually have improved the beach.

In Chapter 6 we will discuss some of the fads that may have done some damage. Performance management fits this category as do various incentive systems which were popular years ago. The damage, or beach erosion, is the long term negative impact created while taking advantage of short term gain. This negative impact is usually in the creation of an antagonistic, rather than supportive, culture. Performance management did improve some areas, but not without establishing a clear Theory X message about management's assumptions about people that created ill feelings that will last a long time. Incentive systems had the same result. The next program you embark on should be preceded by some serious discussion of the desired results on the basis of both short *and* long term.

Think of some of the trends or fads that have had an impact on you and your business over the past few years. For each of them:

- Where are they now?
- What have they left in terms of a cultural shift?
- Are you better off, or worse off?

Here are a few to consider:

- T Groups
- Outdoor based training
- Behavior modification
- Mentoring
- Coaching
- Statistical training
- Team Building
- Transactional analysis
- Work teams
- Career development programs
- Value management

Many trends and fads return several times with new names. Do you know any of these?

Meetings as a Way of
Not Making Decisions

Meetings are sometimes called events where minutes are kept and hours are lost. I once heard it said the meetings were for the purpose of solving problems that we wouldn't have if we didn't have meetings. Sounds like there is a message there somewhere. David Barry in his landmark business book of the century, *Claw Your Way to the Top*, carries this a step farther. He says there are only two forms of work in the modern corporation: taking phone messages for people who are in meetings and going to meetings.

Many mangers find that making decisions is tough. It is much easier to say, "Let's have a meeting on this," than it is to make the decision and get on with the work. Deciding to have a meeting serves as a great substitute for making a real decision. If there is a meeting scheduled on a topic then you don't have to think about it anymore. An extension of this idea is to create a task force—then you have shifted the burden and can really forget about it.

The Two Task Force Extremes

I have seen hundreds of so called task forces, and often wondered how the participants are chosen. I think I know now. There are two categories: Those who have nothing else to do and those who are on every other task force.

The result is always a homogeneous gathering of people who are destined to come out with pretty much the same old answers. The formation of a task force might actually yield some interesting results if whoever put it together recognized that exciting ideas come from an exciting group of people. To create this you should have a mix of people that provides variety of thinking. You should have different levels, ages, sexes, and knowledge backgrounds and include someone who knows absolutely nothing about the subject.

Real creative energy comes from people with different viewpoints. Paul Hawken in his terrific book, *Growing a Business*, coins a new term for this: hybrid vigor. He draws the comparison to the cross breeding of different strains of plants, which results in strong new species. Having people included who have not learned about all the things you *can't* do yet will create a real learning experience for those who have. There will also be commitment to the results at other than the top levels. We could use more hybrid vigor in our task forces.

I am convinced that many of the problems we see today in business and in the private sector result from the guidance provided by incredibly dull boards of directors. I had a chance to observe the activity of a board of directors of a philharmonic orchestra a while back. The fact that it contained a bunch of stodgy, left-brain executives belied the results (or lack of results) it was, and still is able to achieve. The next time you have an opportunity to put together a task force, forget about conventional wisdom and try one that is really different.

The Illusion of Truth—Take Off Your Sweaters

Somewhere there is a connection between truth and the levels of organization. My experience has shown that the lower down in an organization you are, the more honesty and truth there is. That sounds harsh but consider this. As information flows upward about what is really happening in the levels at which people touch product, something happens to this information. Each level passing up information needs to make it sound a little better. Nobody wants to report unfavorable information; it will make them look bad. The result is that the information that reaches the top levels of the hierarchy has little relation to what is really happening at the bottom. I clearly remember a neighbor of mine telling how bad it was in his group and how low the morale was because of all the new programs. In this same group, the managers were giving presentations on how wonderful the new high-performance programs were working. A little genuine managing by wandering around would have given them a clue as to what was really happening.

THE PROJECT

In the beginning was a project, and then the assumptions;

And the project was without form and the assumptions were void;

And the darkness was upon the faces of the implementers;

And they spake unto their manager saying: "It is a crock of shit, and it stinketh";

And the manager went to the 2nd level manager, and he spake unto him saying: "It is a crock of excrement, and none may abide by the odor thereof";

And the 2nd level manager went to the 3rd level manager, and he spake unto him saying: "It is a container of excrement, and it is very strong, such that none may abide before it";

And the 3rd level manager went to the headquarters director, and he spake unto him saying: "It is a vessel of fertilizer, and none may abide by its strength";

And the Director went to the Division Vice President, and he spake unto him saying: "It contains that which aids plant growth, and it is very strong";

And the Vice President went to the Division President, and he spake unto him saying: "It promoteth growth, and it is very powerful";

And the Division President went before the executive board, and he spake unto them saying: "This powerful new project will promote the growth of the company";

And the executive board looked upon the project, and saw it was good.

The illusion of truth is like wearing several layers of sweaters on a cold day. If you have enough sweaters on, you won't have a clue as to the temperature. Similarly, a manager who is shielded by several sweaters of bureaucracy will never really know what's going on in the organization. Bad news that enters at a low level might create a particularly dangerous situation if it is covered up on the way to the top.

I remember my days in the Army when we would have unit inspections. I would prepare my company for inspection using the accepted procedure: making things look good by having the troops load all the unauthorized things into my car. I'm glad the General never looked at my car. Of course, when the inspection was over it was all brought back to the barracks. I thought that was over when I left the Army. Then I realized that the same thing happens when a CEO is coming to visit operating departments of a company. I have seen situations where only his pre-designated route was painted and cleaned up. I've been told of situations where people would ship unauthorized items to their friends in other buildings knowing that, by the time it got delivered and returned, the inspection would be over. If managers made more unannounced inspections they would be much more honestly informed.

The answer these days seems to be having a "flatter" organization. This makes sense until you think of it in terms of the sweater metaphor. It may just mean that the organization is wearing three heavy sweaters rather than five light ones.

Striving for Sameness, and the Inoculation Theory

There seems to be a need for business leaders to create sameness in their organizations. Being different is regarded as being dangerous, a concept that doesn't exactly encourage a lot of creativity. Organizations strive for order, not chaos. And the bigger the organization the more the perceived need for order. When you nurture different points of view you may create chaos, not order. You also stimulate creativity. Since few large organizations are willing to do this, it's no wonder they are rarely able to capture significant creative capability from their associates.

I am reminded of an island of penguins when I think of today's organizations. It's pretty hard to tell one penguin from another. It must be pretty dull. They dress the same, walk the same, and talk the same old penguin talk (whatever *that* is). Take a look around many organizations and you'll see the same thing. People talk the same, look the same and often even walk the same. Sometime when nobody is watching, try to walk your organization's walk. One of my favorite video clips is that of John Cleese in a *Monty Python's Flying Circus* spoof called the Ministry of Silly Walks. I have used this often in workshops as a springboard to help participants recognize their walk and, I hope, begin to change it.

If you inoculate an organization with some people who will create just enough chaos for the system to begin questioning itself, organizational health will improve. As with a medical inoculation, there may be some short term side effects but, over the long term, the body will strengthen. Keep this metaphor in mind as we explore other characteristics of today's organizations.

Winning by Defense

Somewhere in our great business schools it must be taught that good business consists of a series of defensive moves. It just seems that a large number of businesses began with some pretty good offense but, upon winning the first battle, dug in and have been protecting themselves ever since. IBM put their energy into protecting their interests in mainframes and refused to admit there was a potential market for personal computers until it was almost too late. They are still trying to recover and may have forever lost their ability to be great. Kodak was so busy protecting their historically lucrative chemical, film, and paper business that they forgot they were an imaging company and will continue to struggle in the future as imaging shifts to electronic. General Motors refused to let go of their preoccupation with building the cars *they* wanted to build rather than what the customer wanted to buy. The entire railroad industry was so busy defending railroads as they knew them in the past that they let some tremendous opportunities in the transportation business slip away. An opportunity missed often results in a permanent disability rather than just a temporary setback. Many of these companies will never recover from their errors. Once a wimp, always a wimp. Here again, the bigger the business, the more preoccupied it will be with defending its position. When you are tied up with defense, it is difficult to put enough energy into the offense. Football provides an excellent example. Just think of the times when teams have lost in the closing minutes of a game because they decided to play a totally defensive game and forgot about their offense.

When you are busy defending your business, everything that comes at you looks like a threat rather than an opportunity. Treating it as a threat can only result in either making it go away or protecting yourself against it. It can never result in a movement that will build new possibilities for your organization. Joel Barker, in his popular video, *Discovering the Future; The Business of Paradigms*, tells the story of the man who was driving his sports car along a country road and approaching a curve when a car came around the curve careening out of control. As it approached him, a woman yelled from her car, "Pig!" He responded with a few choice words.

Then, as he rounded the curve, he hit the pig. He was responding to what he thought was a threat and she was actually giving him a warning. Are there any threats in your business situation that you could turn to warnings?

This is often called, "playing not to lose" rather than "playing to win" and it is a powerful concept. This idea effectively ties into the use of outdoor challenge courses to firmly implant the concept of winning.

When we concentrate on "not losing," our minds have a tendency to drop the "not." In other words, if we are preoccupied with "not losing" there will be a higher likelihood that our behaviors will result in losing. As an example, what color do you think of when I say to you, "Do not think of blue"? If you didn't think of blue then there is something wrong with you. If you are a golfer and you are telling yourself not to hit the ball in the water or the sand trap, where do you think the ball will go? One of the best business books of this century is Timothy Gallway's *Inner Game of Tennis*. Gallway didn't mean it to be a business book but the ideas he develops in it are quite applicable to what we are talking about here. He suggests that we have a self 1 and a self 2. Our self 1 is constantly talking to us and telling us how to do everything. It is the voice of self 1 that says, "Watch out, don't hit that ball into the net." We all know what happens then. Self 2 is that part of us that is able to do things while drawing on our unconscious capability and our image of success. Most of us would perform much better if we could let go of self 1 and let self 2 do its stuff.

Warren Bennis in his book, *Leaders*, coins a term for this: the Wallenda factor. It relates to the remarkable story of Karl Wallenda who, at age 76, fell to his death from a high wire. He had walked the tightrope nearly all his life and never thought of failing. His wife said later that, prior to the accident, he had mentioned the possibility of falling. In a similar way, companies can plunge to their death if they fear that it will happen. The lesson here is to focus on winning and forget about the possibility of losing. It's hard to lose while you are in the process of winning.

Playing to Lose

On the other hand, playing to lose may be an advantage. Let me explain. For years I have tremendously enjoyed the game of racquetball. I used to think it was important to win, so I would play people I thought I could beat. This does wonders for the win column and the ego but it doesn't do much for improving your game. In racquetball (and other sports) you learn and improve your skills only when you are "playing up." Playing up is another way of saying "playing to lose." If you are not losing at least half the time, you are probably not being challenged enough to learn. The key is in playing an opponent who will challenge you to stretch yourself, but who can occasionally be beaten. However, playing an opponent who is far better and impossible to beat only results in frustration.

The notion of being number one is also an interesting one to challenge. There is a downside to being number one. There is nobody out in front of you—no one to overcome—which may bring on complacency. Racing supplies an analogy. In some ways, the second car has a distinct advantage over the one in the lead. The second place driver can see clearly what he needs to beat whereas the driver of the car in front is always looking behind and thinking of protecting his lead. And the driver in second place can take advantage of the leader's draft to provide a little extra pull that, when needed, may help to propel him into the winner's spot. There is also the thought that vision is clearer while looking forward than it is looking back. Observing the competition from behind allows you a clear view of their every move. Very few large companies ever "blindside" their smaller competition which is not true in the reverse. Observing number one from behind allows a clear view of any empty spaces they may leave which might mean tremendous opportunities for you.

If You Can't Measure it, It's Probably Important

There is an assumption in many business circles that the only things worthwhile are those things that can be measured. My sense is that just the opposite is more often true, although measurability or lack of it are certainly not sole determinants of importance. Many of today's "programs" produce this need for measurability along with a false sense of comfort because we have something to measure. The truth is that this often results in "looking good without being good."

I once consulted in a staff organization that supplied some very powerful material to internal consultants within a major company. Our job was to develop new material and transfer it to other consultants. We were also called upon to provide consulting when experts were needed. With that short description in mind, would you care to guess what one of the major measures of success was? It was based on how many floppy discs they recycled during the year! Surely, this group was doing something more important than this. But, it was easy to measure. The question I ask is, "What do people think when their leaders are celebrating how many floppy discs were recycled and ignoring the real accomplishments?"

Some of the most important long-term keys to business success are very difficult to measure. Items such as strength of the learning organization, capabilities in the core competencies, capacity to use creativity, amount of caring about each other, morale, ability to listen with empathy, mentoring capability, and conversational abilities are but a few. None of these can be measured with any degree of success but they are all vital to an organization's future.

Concentrating on those things which are easily measurable is bad for a couple of reasons. First, it takes energy which is then unavailable for other things that may be more important. It takes energy to create and operate a measuring system. It also wastes energy for those who are being measured (against criteria that are likely not important to them) to "fudge" the figures so they can look good and get back to what they perceive as important. It also has the tendency to send the wrong message about what is important. If you are measuring rather insignificant, but easily measurable, factors in the workplace, you are suggesting *that* is what is important to you. You may also be overlooking the things that are really vital.

One of the more interesting, informal measures of work in many organizations is the number of people that work longer than necessary hours. The assumption tends to be that, if people are working long hours, they must really love what they are doing and be doing a good job. In reality, many of these people are just hoping others (especially the boss) will leave so they can too. After many years of working long hours it suddenly dawned on me that my best work was done while I was not at work. Those who are really interested in their work carry it around with them all the time. And the most creative ideas tend to come when you get away from the normal work environment and "let go."

Acronymania

Organizations create their own language. I remember when I started my first job—thinking that I had landed on another planet after listening to the strange language. There are so many acronyms used in organizations that the uninitiated have a difficult time carrying out a conversation. People pride themselves on their ability to conjure up new acronyms for teams, task forces, products, and information systems. I remember a few acronyms that didn't experience much success. A company division was renamed United States Equipment Division, a short lived name when someone realized its acronym wasn't appropriate (USED). A new machine designed to provide doctors with quick blood analysis in their office was going to be called "Doctor's Office Assistant" until they realized that DOA would not be a great selling acronym.

You may get the impression that I am anti-acronym which is not the case. I think acronyms can be used quite effectively to enhance an organization's environment. If they are not overused and are chosen wisely they can produce positive energy in the workplace.

This New Program is Really Something

Those responsible for initiating new programs, whether internal staff groups or outside consultants, have a remarkable capacity to prove how well their program is working. I have never seen a situation in which the originators of a program could take an objective viewpoint of its results. There is a strong incentive to prove that your ideas are working well. After all, admitting anything other than total success is usually too risky. A terrible program coupled with some strong-willed drivers who can convince a few levels that it is really working has a good chance for survival. Some wonderful, well thought out, creative, risky approaches that are harder to communicate and don't show clear short-term gains might never get off the ground.

To find the truth regarding how well some of these programs are working it is necessary to ask those who are *not* directly involved. If you want to know the true feeling for a

Total Quality Management program ask "grass roots" people. You will likely get an answer much different from the one provided to you by the Quality Department. Yet, management usually makes its judgments based on what they hear from a handful of people who are stakeholders in a program's success and not necessarily the success of the company. Those who's success depends upon the success of the programs they perpetuate will go out of their way to claim, and prove, how great they are. The result may be a disaster that sounds wonderful.

Search for the Holy Grail

Internal and external consultants seem to thrive on having *the* answer. Drop everything else—my program is all you need. Perhaps that is one reason why there is a tendency to be engaged in a constant search for that all-embracing system that will solve all the company's problems. Actually, what you are looking for is contained in this book. (Sorry—I felt compelled to say that and I am only kidding—sort of.) The truth is that there is no cure-all to solve all the problems of business. And, if you think you have found it in the form of Total Quality Management, a learning organization, reengineering, or some other great program, think again. If you have settled on a program that you think has all the answers, you have become too comfortable. Achieving great futures is a constant pursuit where the process and the results you vision are always changing.

Let's Have Another Survey

The use (or misuse) of formal surveys is one of the great energy wasters that comes in response to business downturns. Right after the decision to reorganize comes the decision to make a survey. Let's survey our customers, employees, suppliers, etc. These surveys usually are in lieu of having managers actually get out and talk with people. They are also very expensive and inaccurate. They serve as a way to avoid eyeball-to-eyeball discussion—which is where the real value is. And, when the survey data is in, there are countless hours spent in meetings discussing what they mean, setting up defense systems, and rejecting most of the data as meaningless.

Do I sound like I am down on formal surveys? I am! Surveys, in the form of continual conversation with customers, employees, and suppliers, is something that should be taking place in the context of the work all the time. The only way to get honest feedback about how well you are doing in a business is to have honest and open relationships and dialogue with all the players. Hiding behind a formal survey will only result in your getting inaccurate information too late to do you any good.

Seek Simplicity—Then Distrust it

This quotation from Alfred North Whithead has always intrigued me. Maybe it is my simple mind, but I tend to strongly favor simplicity in the processes that orchestrate results in an organization. Complexity has a way of increasing exponentially as it works its way through the cranial areas within organizations. The simple fact is that work gets done through a series of conversations between people. The more complex the material that must be passed on, the higher the probability it will be misinterpreted. We need to concentrate on eliminating the complex processes that bog organizations down. I am not suggesting that individuals are not capable of complex thought processes. Many people pride themselves on their ability to think complex thoughts and this is OK. But the string of thought in an organization has to be connected by some simply stated commonalties.

Let's Study it More

I recently heard reference to a study made for the Fragrance Institute. The findings supported the feelings that some people in the Fragrance Institute had that fragrance was going to be very important in the future. I thought to myself, "What a surprise!" If those who had made the study had come out with an opposite result they probably would have been fired. The point is that we have the power to prove anything we want with a study—and usually we do. Engaging in studies is often a waste of time. It is an excuse for not doing anything or the net result of failure to make a decision. Many managers feel comfortable when the action taken on a problem is to study it more. After all, you are off the hook for a while. Perhaps the problem will go away during the study. But studies tie up people. It scares me to think about all the people hours that I have seen spent on useless studies. The really frightening part is that so many of these studies resulted in—you guessed it—more studies. And they always generate more meetings.

We have not learned to use the intuitive decision-making capabilities of our managers. It may help us avoid the work that can result from a lack of decision making. For some reason we have encouraged managers to gather a tremendous amount of data to support decision making. And it is so easy to say that you don't have enough data. I am certainly not suggesting blind decision making but I think there is plenty of room for quicker decisions with fewer data-producing studies. Then we can get on with the work of the organization instead of side tracking our energy on wasteful activities.

Benchmarking

I used to think that benchmarking was a concept that described what my dog did when I took her to a park. American industry seems to be having a love affair with the idea of benchmarking. Benchmarking is, quite clearly, a reactive and responsive orientation to managing which is like playing a game of leapfrog. We'll see what our competitors are doing, then we can determine how to "jump over them." More important, we should be benchmarking ourselves against the possibilities—and not against what others have done. This is not the case for a number of those engaging in benchmarking. Most benchmarking activities result in improvement, but only that which makes you just as good (or only slightly better than) the competition. Benchmarking rarely creates breakthrough because it doesn't set sights high enough. The best benchmarking forgets about the competition and looks at how well we are doing and what the possibilities are in the future.

Several companies have used benchmarking effectively but I have seen some awful cases of "me-tooism" that have spun off from these studies. They create a "playing not to lose" atmosphere which prevents a company from achieving real breakthrough. The energy and resources consumed in benchmarking studies can be tremendous. Diverting your energy to looking at the other guys may just give the other guys a better chance to beat you.

People as Costs Rather than Resources

It is popular for companies to say that people are their most important resource. When the rubber hits the road and the economy tests how valid this is, they often revert to lay-offs. This suggests that people are considered as costs of doing business rather than as resources for producing business.

55

Accountants can easily attach dollar values to buildings and tools but haven't the slightest notion how to bring the value of people and core competencies into view. We need to change this mindset to one which clearly identifies the value of people and core competencies that they provide the business and places it at a high level of importance in business decisions.

Training: A Reward or an Enhancer of Core Competence?

There is a proliferation of training seminars and, if my mail box is any indication of its direction, it is growing like mad. I am talking about the $49 to $99 per day variety where several hundred people are packed into a room to listen to a professional lecturer who, quite often, knows nothing at all about the topic. These seminars are, for the most part, a total waste of time and money. Ironically, the attendees often love them. Why? Because it gives them a chance to get away for a day, and they are under the illusion that they will learn something. The boss usually feels good about it too because a training request has been fulfilled and it didn't cost much. There are some outstanding training and development activities available but, in this area, you truly get what you pay for. Beware of low-cost seminars which travel around the country appealing to mass audiences. You'd be better off giving your employees a day off to read a good book.

Thought Provokers Concerning Managerial Illusions

1. Which of the illusions discussed in this chapter sound familiar to you?

2. What trends and fads have been practiced by your company?

    Which have had positive effects?

    Which have had negative effects?

3. In what ways might you shift your thinking regarding the illusions that sound familiar to you?

4. Do you have a "play to win" atmosphere in your company?

5. Which of these illusions would have the greatest impact if you could make significant shifts in how you think about them?

6. Do you feel you can have an influence on these thinking shifts? What are you waiting for?

Chapter 4

Thinking Outside the Organization's Box

"The world that we have made as a result of the level of thinking we have done thus far creates problems that we cannot solve at the same level at which we created them."— Albert Einstein

Getting Hooked on Paradigms

Someone once said, "There are two types of people, those who separate things into pairs and those who don't." At this point there are probably two types of people in organizations, those who have never heard the word "paradigm" and those who can't complete a sentence without including the word. It's a strange word. It tends to hook people. And its meaning is fuzzy enough so that it leaves lots of room for misuse. Paradigms are simply rules, patterns, or assumptions through which we filter incoming information. We see the world through our paradigms. The word was first explored by Thomas Kuhn in *The Structure of Scientific Revolutions* to explain the patterns of thinking that affect a scientist's ability to discover. He suggested that these paradigms blocked scientists' ability to see keys to discovery that were outside their normal view. Stephen Covey and Joel Barker popularized the word and carried it outside the boundaries of scientific thought. Most organizations contain thickets of paradigms which keep employees from beating a path to discovery.

I have helped hundreds of groups explore the negative effects of paradigms and have found it to be a powerful step toward achieving breakthrough in thinking. To strive for creativity and breakthrough without first trying to discover how paradigms influence your thinking is like trying to eat with your teeth clenched. The only things that get in are the things that can squeeze between the teeth. Maybe that's why so many things coming out of businesses look like dental floss.

Characteristics of Paradigms

Paradigms influence people's thoughts and, therefore, what they do. They tend to become self-fulfilling prophecies. For example, if my paradigm about leadership in an organization tells me that there are people who lead and people who follow, I will tend not to assume any leadership traits if I perceive myself as a follower. That will reinforce my co-workers' perception that I am a follower, and my behavior will not change. If something causes me to realize that I can exert leadership, I will begin to behave as a leader and, therefore, may become one. Imagine the possibilities in a workplace when there are real shifts in the paradigms that relate to how we view empowerment. Those companies that have developed strong work systems have made significant shifts in their paradigms of people at work. Many companies have tried and failed to create empowered work systems simply because they were never able to shift their workplace paradigms.

In Joel Barker's video, *Discovering the Future; The Business of Paradigms,* he uses an example of a Mexican Indian tribe whose members go for 70-mile runs. They apparently haven't heard that the ultimate marathon is 26 miles. We all put limits on our capabilities and, in business we have placed many artificial constraints on our capabilities. Are there any areas in your situation where you have defined the limits of your possibility?

Because paradigms block our field of view, we have a difficult time seeing things that our paradigms don't support. In many cases, we are totally blind to possibilities outside this field of view! We can't see them, we can't verbalize them, we can't write them and, if they smelled, we couldn't smell them. I am reminded of race horses that wear blinders so they won't be able to see anything except that which is directly in front of them. Many organizations can be pictured as having people wearing blinders. The difference is that, in organizations, most people are looking backward.

Paradigms tend to turn the old adage, "I'll believe that when I see it," into "I'll see that when I believe it."

Paradigm Stories

Sony Corporation, well known for its innovation and new-product development, was doing research and development on compact-disc audio and video systems in the early eighties. Their video program was doing well but their audio program had reached an impasse and was temporarily halted. Fortunately for us, Phillips was also engaged in developing audio disks and decided to get together with the folks at Sony to talk about standards. When the discussion came to the standard for the size of the disc it became clear that Sony had been stalled in their program by their inability to see beyond a very simple paradigm. Music is on a 12-inch disc, and a 12-inch compact disc can hold nearly 18 hours of music. They were stalled because it didn't occur to them to make the disc smaller. How many engines does a car have? Our current paradigm would tell us a car is supposed to have just one engine. The engineers at Audi shifted this paradigm and out came the possibility of a car with both an electric and a gasoline engine: gas for long trips and electric for short. And you won't have to worry about charging if running on gas will charge the electric system.

How do we reduce noise in automobiles? Our normal paradigms tell us this is done by muffling it in some way (sound insulating material, mufflers) or by reducing the noise by more expensive machining of parts. Lotus Engineering made a shift in these paradigms and looked at it from a different angle. Noise is in the form of a wave which can be theoretically canceled by an opposite wave. They developed a system that can measure the noise and generate a canceling wave that results in suppressed noise in the car's interior—an electronic solution to a problem previously believed to be mechanical.

Some paradigms were developed years ago for reasons forgotten or obsolete. Almost everyone is familiar with the word, QWERTYUIOP. If you are not, it is the top line of letters on a normal typewriter keyboard. This layout has been the standard for the past 100 years, even though it is inefficient. The configuration was done to reduce the number of times that two adjacent mechanical keys would be struck at the same time and perhaps cause a hang-up. Mechanical keys have been gone a long time but we are having a hard time shifting to a new configuration.

Years ago, the handle of a tennis racket went from round to eight sided. Nobody knows why the eight-sided shape was selected. Nobody questioned it until an inventor from Cleveland, an actuary by trade, determined that a six-sided handle was superior. The stress on the arm is reduced and it has been shown to improve a forehand shot by 14% after only 15 minutes of practice.

The first nails (from Mesopotamia) date to 3500 BC. Since the mid 1800s, nails have been mass produced by machines in basically the same form as today. An inventor from Florida makes a convincing argument that his nails, that are star shaped in their cross section, are far superior. They have much more friction surface and are less apt to split the wood. How dare someone question something as simple and traditional as the common nail. And, finally, the shape of a refrigerator has been basically the same as long as I can remember. Its "box" shape probably comes from the days of "ice boxes" and blocks of ice. Electrolux has recently been developing a vertical, cylindrical refrigerator. Just think of the possibilities.

Why did it take so long to think of a new shape for something as common as a refrigerator?

Do you know of something in your field of view that might be questioned? What characteristics of common products or services, if shifted, would result in some real innovation?

Some paradigms involve assumptions about the workplace. The word "love" has never been associated with work. *Do What You Love and the Money Will Follow* and *Love and Profit* suggest a shift is talking place. Could it be possible that we could love our work and love the people we work with in the future? What are the implications of this?

Many companies are willing to spend money to train people and allow them to receive higher education as long as it is in their field of expertise. At least one company, 3M, has recognized the value of education *outside* a person's normal profession, and has eliminated that constraint. Remember, much of the creative discovery comes from knowledge that exists outside the normal boundaries. I see some powerful shifts occurring when we get beyond the normal paradigm that learning has to be centered on the employee's current job requirements and support learning for the love of learning.

When I started my first job as an Industrial Engineer I was given a huge stack of policy manuals to read. Over the years there has been a steady decline in the thickness of policy manuals, which might be considered steady improvement but not a paradigm shift. Norstrand Company has a policy manual that is just two sentences long. "All employees will use their best judgment" and "There are no other policies." Now *that's* a paradigm shift.

When Steelcase was building its new corporate office they reviewed some of the normal design assumptions. One assumption was that office space should be designed so that people could move around comfortably without bothering each other. Then someone said, "Why are we trying to keep people away from each other? That's where the action is." They decided to design the area so that people would have to run into each other and coined the words "functional non-adjacency" to describe their approach. Today their Corporate Pyramid is a model of an effective paradigm shift in design. The next time you are involved in a design problem, ask yourself what paradigms you can shift to create new possibilities.

Famous Fools

Paradigm shifters are frequently well outside of the boundaries and are often considered fools for their ridiculous ideas. We assume that those who have the answers are our leaders and our intellectual superiors. To illustrate how invalid this is, consider the following quotations:

"There is no reason for any individual to have a computer in their home."—Ken Olson. President of Digital Equipment Company, 1977.

"We don't like their sound. Besides, guitar groups are on the way out."—President of Decca Records as he turned down the Beatles in 1962.

"The Japanese auto industry is not likely to carve out a big slice of the US. market for itself."—*Business Week*, August 2, 1968.

"The phonograph is not of any commercial value."—Thomas Edison, inventor of the phonograph, 1880.

"Everything that can be invented has been invented."—Charles Duell, Director of US. Patent Office, 1899.

"Sensible and responsible women do not want to vote."—Grover Cleveland, 1905.

A few years ago there was a popular bumper sticker that implored us to "Question authority." Perhaps that is a wise choice. The questioning of authority can be done in a very gentle and unthreatening manner. The next time someone with authority makes a statement that is limiting, like the above examples, play with the reverse of the statement a while and see what happens.

Since we tend to think that all of the answers reside within our own community, we have difficulty accepting outsiders with paradigm shifting ideas. We consider them to be fools, which means there are a lot of rich and famous fools around. Consider a few of these "famous fools."

Alexander Graham Bell was considered a fool by many and an idiot by some. Yet his inventions stand as ringing reminders of his contributions in the communication field.

George Westinghouse was called a fool when he promised to stop railroad trains with compressed air.

The inventor of the TV, Philo Farnsworth, could not get a patent for his invention in his own country.

Bill Bowerman, a coach and founder of Nike, tried to get some sneaker manufacturers interested in his new sneaker design and was told, "We don't tell you how to coach and you don't tell us how to make shoes." Bill discovered his design while eating waffles (next time you have waffles place your sneakers upside down next to your plate and you see why).

Allen Breed invented a new triggering device for auto-safety air bags based on his knowledge of manufacturing hand grenades. When he approached the major automobile companies to tell them about it, what do you think they told him?

And there is always the Chester Carlson story. Having invented a new imaging system in the 1930s, he proceeded to try and sell his process which formed images by using static electricity and black powder to companies like Kodak who were making images with chemicals. He was promptly shown to the door. After all, someone outside the imaging business couldn't possibly know enough to create a new imaging system. Louis Jaque Mande Daquerre, inventor of the first practical photographic imaging system was a famous mural painter. It's ironic that nearly 20 years after Kodak's faux pas Xerox would reject Steve Jobs' suggestion to develop the personal computer as "too risky." Of course, he went on to form Apple Computer Company which later rejected another outsider's opinion for a new operating system. That outsider was Bill Gates, who went on to form Microsoft. Think again the next time you're ready to reject someone as an outsider. A speaker at a recent World Future Society conference on the future of business told a story about some aliens who visited Earth to observe us Earthlings for a while. When they returned home they reported that Earth was inhabited by things called automobiles, each of which had its own slave. The slaves periodically wash their automobiles, feed them and take them for drives. The point of her story was that we may need to look at things through "alien eyes" every now and then if we want to create breakthrough futures.

Managers often give the most difficult problems to the most experienced people. There is a problem hidden in this thinking. Those people who have been around long enough to build an experience base have also been around long enough to be blinded by their paradigms. The next time you are up against something that is "impossible" you may want to give it to the new kid on the block. There is a good possibility this person hasn't yet learned all the reasons why it can't be done.

Key Paradigm Questions

Paradigms exist in all walks of life and all areas of business. Organizations are forests of paradigms. To raise the possibility of creating a breakthrough future, you must identify the thinking patterns that are holding you back. Then you can shift them. There are some difficult questions to tackle that will require some stretch thinking. An outside facilitator may be very helpful in the questioning process to assure that you are really challenging your thinking. Here's your chance to use "alien eyes" to understand how others really view you.

1. What paradigms influence how we think about our work? It may be worthwhile to focus on some specific areas such as:

- the business itself
- the manufacturing process
- research and development
- the competition
- our resources and suppliers
- people
- the technologies
- the environment
- community relations

2. What would outsiders say our paradigms are?

- customers
- competitors
- work force
- suppliers
- the community

3. What things are impossible today but, if possible, would fundamentally shift how we do business? This is a powerful question and also a difficult one. Remember, if you think it's

impossible, you may not even be able to see it. You'll need to work hard to get answers, but it is well worth the trouble.

4. List some things we currently think of as threats. How might we think of these as opportunities instead? A major blockage can occur when we put most of our energy into protecting ourselves from perceived threats rather than creating new things. If you are honest with yourself, this question may help you uncover some interesting possibilities.

5. What are some of your own personal paradigms? How do they influence your ability to uncover organizational paradigms?

6. Are there any jargon terms that tend to tightly frame your picture of possibilities? This question may uncover hidden possibilities. Virtually every item has one or more descriptors that lock you into a vision of what that item is. In other words, the words create the paradigm and limit your ability to create something different. When we hear the word "clock" we get a picture of a clock. Shifting to the word "timekeeper" will allow us to expand our possibilities about products for keeping time.

These questions will help you explore the paradigms that are important to you. To make this a successful exercise, you must identify statements that are blocking your potential and identify the possibilities that come from reversing them.

To create paradigm shifts it is important to master the art of "forgetting." Einstein once said, "The world that we have made as a result of the level of thinking we have done thus far creates problems that we cannot solve at the same level at which we created them." Analogies are a powerful tool for helping us think outside our normal patterns so, lets take a look at some analogies for organizations.

Chapter 5

Games and Other Interesting Analogies for Organizations

"It takes a long time to grow young."—
Picasso

Work as an Extension of our Childhood Games

As you have seen, I tend to use analogies to try to make sense of current situations. I find there are some interesting parallels between childhood games and the behaviors that people display at work. Some of us are still playing those games. Let me give you a few examples.

I am sure you can recall the game of dodgeball, the popular game in which we all learned how to escape challenges that were thrown our way. The person who was "it" was circled by the rest of the kids and the object was to dodge the ball that the group was trying to hit him with. This is where the term, "dodging responsibility" originated. Today's organizations are full of people who are either trying not to be "it" or, if they are "it," are busily trying to dodge things that are thrown at them. I remember the long summer nights when the neighborhood kids would entertain themselves for hours playing kick-the-can. This was basically a creative version of hide-and-seek wherein the person who was "it" would cover his eyes and to give others time to hide themselves. Then, he would call, "Ready or not, here I come!" as he starts out to find them. A can was placed at "home." He would begin trying to capture the others who would be corralled near the can but, if someone who had not been found yet could sneak up and kick the can, all prisoners were released. In what ways is the behavior of people at work similar to a game of kick the can?

- People at work tend to enjoy kicking the cans out from under their compatriots in the form of killing their ideas, eroding their support, or withholding their feelings.
- When the can is kicked we all run for cover while "it" retrieves the can.
- If the can is not kicked far enough away, the players may not be able to escape without being caught.
- You will be highly motivated to get back at someone who "kicked your can" later.

I could continue this but I think you get the point.

The ultimate game of my childhood was one we made up ourselves. We called it "muckle." There were very simple rules. A football was laid in the middle of the yard and the first boy who dared to pick it up and run with it was immediate fair game for the rest of the boys (I guess Rugby is close). The idea was to jump on the kid who had the ball, and this is not too far from what we do in business these days. The person who takes a chance and tries something new had better be ready for the attack.

Role Creation in our Childhood Games

To the extent that we have learned roles as children, we have carried these roles into the workplace. If you were a boy, you played cops-and-robbers or cowboys-and-Indians or something similar. You learned that there were bad guys and good guys and you probably think that is still true. If you were a girl you played with Barbie and it strengthened your perception of the role of women at that time. Maybe that is why it is so difficult to change in today's world to a much more realistic model of diversity in the workplace. The men are still playing cops-and-robbers and think that the women should be playing with their Barbie dolls.

Business Meetings—The Ultimate Game of Poker

Somewhere in my distant past I remember playing Poker with "the boys." The winners were usually those who had a good combination of luck, skill, and the ability to maintain a good "poker face." As a matter of fact, many games required us to use these poker faces so our opponent wouldn't know what we were thinking. We continue to disguise our real feelings in work-related situations just as we have learned in these games. How often have you resorted to the use of a poker face to disguise the hand you were holding in a business situation? How often have you been totally in the dark about how someone you were dealing with really was feeling about something that was going on?

For some reason, there seems to be a great deal of resistance to bringing feelings and emotion into the workplace. We assume that feelings and emotion are things that need to be left at home and dealt with only on personal time. As a result, many workplaces have become emotionally sterile areas that have the capability of accommodating only a small percentage of a person's mental and emotional capacity. The inability of people to express their real feelings in the workplace imposes a severe limitation on their ability to achieve breakthrough. True commitment comes when people are totally involved in their work, and total involvement means the whole self, including feelings and emotions.

Nature's Analogies for the Organization

I consider myself a Creative-Process Consultant because I have spent many years helping to bring out the best in the creativity of people at work. Creativity draws heavily upon the infinite supply of nature analogies because they supply rich triggers for new thinking. Nature provides a wonderful and endless source of material that helps us get outside our normal thinking boxes. It also provides new thinking for our businesses and organizations. And you sure don't need to look far to find good examples. Just think about the things that exist around you, browse through a magazine, take a walk, or pick from this list:

• human body	• trees
• perennials	• streams
• mountains	• icebergs
• birds	• volcanoes
• lobsters	• snakes
• grass	• oceans
• spider plants	• coal mines
• fish	• body organs
• deserts	• forests

Let's look at a few of these analogies.

Grass as a Fertile Analogy

Look out the window. If you are lucky, you see grass, trees, soil, flowers, and birds. If you see only asphalt and cars, pretend you see something else. Focus on the grass for a moment and think about some of its characteristics.

The question to keep in mind is, "What does grass have in common with organizations, and what lessons can we learn from how grass connects to its environment?"

- The best grass is a diverse mixture of high quality grasses.
- When sowing new grass it is wise to add some annual rye grass to pave the way for the more permanent types.
- Grass grows best when it is cut frequently.
- Weeds grow in grass that is not healthy and thick.
- The soil has much to do with the ultimate health of the grass.
- Fertilizer is needed regularly to keep the grass healthy.
- Grass must be kept in check or it will invade areas where you don't want it.
- Grass keeps soil from eroding.
- Grass is slippery when wet.
- Mown grass serves as marvelous fertilizer for existing grass.

We could go on endlessly. I hope my point is clear. If you take each one of these characteristics and ask what the similarity is between it and your business organization you will be able to change the way you think. You may also find yourself having a lot of fun.

Roots and Shoots

Consider the analogy between a tree and an organization.

- A tree has an intricate network of roots that seek water and nourishment.
- Shoots that work their way along the surface are very tender and yet can force their way through concrete.
- The age of a tree is shown by its rings.
- The tree has a main trunk, off-shoot trunks, and branches.

- Leaves and flowers grow, then die when the season is over.
- Insects love trees. There is a whole world of insect life in most trees.
- The tree has a protective bark.
- When the tree is big enough, it can be cut into pieces and sold as firewood or lumber.
- Trees provide great nesting places for birds.
- One good chain saw can take down a mighty oak.
- Pruning may make a tree look good but, overdone, it may kill the tree.

What are some of the implications of the tree analogies to your business? The next time you have a dialogue about your organization, start by using this analogy and see the rich new thinking that appears.

Icebergs

Thinking about organizations as icebergs has provided me with some rich dialogue on a number of occasions. Only a small percentage of an iceberg is above water. It's the large mass concealed below water that tends to keep the iceberg from doing anything exciting. Isn't this true of most organizations as well? A very small portion of an organization reveals itself to us and this is a product of the large cultural mass driving it. A discussion of how to create breakthrough in organizations wouldn't be complete if we only inspect that portion above the surface. It's the portion below the surface that keeps the organization from moving forward.

You need to trim this portion but not eliminate it. If an iceberg had nothing below the surface it would be unstable and that is certainly true of an organization. We must analyze and map the mass below the surface. Then we'll be able to re-shape it, perhaps more like a boat hull, so we can more readily steer our corporate berg toward our goal. In other words, by using this analogy you can identify and shape a culture that will allow a learning organization to grow.

Talk to the Animals

The animal world provides endless analogies to help us understand behaviors in the workplace. Warren Thomas's 1990 book, *Dolphin Conferences, Elephant Midwives, and Other Astonishing Facts About Animals*, provides some examples of animal behaviors that trigger interesting implications for organizations. How might you compare your organization to:

- A school of fish? Note the similarities to the patterns of organizational leadership.
- Humpback whales?
- Bees and birds (as opposed to birds and bees)?
- Dogs and cats?

The Organization as a Human Body

The human body is a remarkable piece of work which provides us with a terrific model for the design of organizations. What is the heart of an organization and what are some of the characteristics of a human heart that can help us in the design of a breakthrough organization? What can we learn from the digestive system that would help us understand more creative ways to process material within our organization? What creative discussions might come about if you thought about the organizational tract and the flow of information as if it were following this path. Could your reengineering programs benefit from looking at something like the human body which happens to be pretty well engineered in the beginning? How might we create faster movement and response in the organization by using the body's brain, nerve, and muscle connections as a model? What possibilities are provided if we look for links between a body's reproductive system and the future needs of an organization?

These are just a few questions to encourage your desire to explore this topic. You see, you don't need to have an "out of body" experience to enter the exciting world of creative inquiry.

Thought Provokers on Games
and Other Interesting Analogies

1. What are some games you remember from your childhood and what are the relationships to your work today?

2. What shifts in these behaviors might create a higher probability of breakthrough in your organization?

3. What is your favorite animal and what specific traits distinguish it? How are these traits similar to your experiences at work?

4. Think of a particular aspect of nature. Identify some things that are true about what you have chosen. What is the connection to your work?

5. Are you enjoying this? If you think it is fun doing it all by your self, try it with a few others.

Chapter 6

Miscellaneous Irreverence

"Just cause everything has changed doesn't mean anything is different."—Alfred E. Newman

Observations from Outside
the Organizational Fishbowl

In 27 years of consulting I've spent a considerable amount of time making third-party observations. The dynamics within organizations are truly fascinating and some of the most highly touted processes are often creating roadblocks to breakthrough and transformation rather than promoting them. The following are some observations that may surprise you. You may also disagree with some of them but, remember, an open mind can pave the way to breakthrough.

Performance Management—
The Fad That Ate The Company

Some fads run their courses and do no harm—perhaps even leave a little bit of good in their wake. There are some, however, that I feel damage the internal culture and health of an organization. They leave hard feelings, misunderstandings, harmful relationships and perceptions that may take years to overcome. I know there will be people who will disagree with me on this, perhaps violently, but Performance Management (PM) falls into this category. Fueled by consultants and the promise of short-term change, PM is a process based firmly in Theory X. It has the capacity to alienate everyone in an organization beyond the few staff and line people who are convinced that it is the best thing they have ever seen to increase performance.

There is no argument that PM can produce gains in the short term. There are many examples of this, usually written by those who have been involved in PM projects and genuinely feel they are working. These projects succeeded, most often, in companies that were so bad off that *anything* would have worked. In many of these PM programs, the gains may be the result of the "Hawthorn effect." This suggests that just paying attention to people who are not used to having anyone show interest in their work will have a short-term positive effect. The key question is: "Are the gains worth the sacrifice of a long-term culture which can produce high performance from within?" I don't believe that a company willing to subscribe to a process that has its roots in behavioral studies of pigeons and dogs is really interested in the creation of a high performance environment, anyway.

In the long run, people are motivated by factors that are intrinsic to their work and workplace. To the extent that they are stimulated by their work and work relationships, they will perform their best. It is not quite as simple as that, but it's close. Performance Management is motivation by external force as opposed to the more desirable approach of motivating from within. For those who are not familiar with PM, let me give you a quick explanation. PM is the scientific use of rewards to motivate people. At one time it was referred to as *behavior modification*, which was a more accurate description. However, BM just didn't seem like a very classy acronym although it may have better expressed the feeling of those on the receiving end of the process. So what is wrong with PM? Lets take a close look at some of its faults.

The main problem is that it perpetuates Theory X culture. It is based on the assumption that people are motivated externally, either by reward or punishment (the carrot or the stick). Once you have convinced everyone that this is the paradigm of leadership, you will forfeit the tremendous possibilities that can be gained by the intrinsic approaches that come from Theory Y assumptions—those that assume people are motivated from within. A decision to manage based on Theory X results in the self-fulfilling prophecy that creates people who will behave correctly only when there is a carrot or stick involved.

The process works by finding particular behaviors that you want to change (called pinpoints) and identifying measures for these. Unfortunately, most of the behaviors that should really be rewarded are not very measurable. The result is that most PM programs focus on meaningless, but easily measurable, pinpoints. These are rarely connected to what people really perceive as important in their work. And they divert attention from the things that are important as well. People can develop a distaste for their work if they lack good, genuine feedback about what they feel is important—particularly if they are getting feedback about some useless measure that just happens to fit the program. Overall performance can't be adequately measured by one or two pinpoints anyway.

Many PM programs are accompanied by heavy training schedules to indoctrinate everyone. Besides taking time from some valuable work, these programs have the effect of alienating a substantial part of the work force. People put up with them because they tend to be entertaining. They find a certain sense of enjoyment watching their managers make fools of themselves. And they usually get a free T-shirt and hat, and some time away from their jobs.

PM comes from a reactive orientation. The measures are always related to problem solving rather than creating possibility. People can achieve tremendous breakthrough in their work, but PM holds them back and wastes their energy on things that feed the program rather than things that create breakthrough.

Any program designed to manipulate people using external factors will generate a strong motivation to make the measurements come out right. In the days of incentive programs people would develop incredibly creative processes to make the numbers come out to standards. PM is an incentive program and the same dynamics will trap people into making things *look* good rather than actually making them good. I have seen some very creative schemes for making figures come out right in these programs. If only that creativity could be put to use doing something valuable!

The Art of Complaining

Have you ever gone through an entire day without hearing someone complain? It's almost become an art form. Have you ever been through a day without complaining yourself? (Be honest now.) It's hard to be happy about everything in our lives. I think we complain because it makes us feel better. The problem is that we rarely complain to the right people and we rarely look at ourselves as being the one to change the things we don't like. After we have complained to someone, we feel we have done our job and we can stop worrying about that particular issue for a while. Unfortunately, since nothing has really changed, we will need to do some more complaining soon. Good complainers become professional "whiners" and tend to spend a large part of their day practicing their art.

I have used "whining sessions" in a number of my workshops and found it to be very therapeutic. When people are dealing with change, it helps to give them time to mourn the past. Whining can be a good release. The important thing is to make sure that whining, or complaining, is not looked on as an end result. The result needs to be action toward creating something that takes you beyond the situation that created the complaint.

The Not-Invented-Here Syndrome

I have come to believe that "not invented here" (NIH) is one of the most powerful dynamics in the workplace (and beyond). It is responsible for a tremendous amount of wasted energy for a number of reasons:

- Projects struggle because they have no support from those who were not the "inventors."

- Efforts are duplicated because people need to "do their own thing."

- Pointless programs are established to satisfy the needs of some individuals to have their own approaches in place.

One way to get beyond this problem is by creating an environment that truly supports team behavior. This is often not easy to do since you will need to overcome some natural NIH tendencies to create such a team. And, in the process of building the team, there is always a strong possibility that the team itself will end up with an NIH orientation of its own. Within a team, this may be a more powerful force than it is with individuals.

Getting Ahead by Making Others Look Bad

There are many ways to get ahead in this world. Unfortunately, one of those ways is to look better by making others look worse. When is the last time you went out of your way to make a peer look good? Providing real support to others in the workplace is much too rare. In my years of experience I have only know a handful of people who genuinely tried to make others look good. In all cases, these were people who were so good themselves that they didn't need to worry about making others look bad.

Lack of Feedback in Organizations

The word "feedback" was popular back in the early 1970s when I was heavily involved in the early stages of Organizational Development. In many of the team building sessions we would help people give each other feedback. I didn't realize then how important, and how lacking, this feedback was. I am amazed at how seldom people give meaningful feedback. "Meaningful feedback" occurs when you learn something constructive about the results of your behavior. We need to know what results we have generated so we can maintain or change our course of action.

Operating without feedback is like running through the woods on a moonless night. You keep bumping into things because you can't see the path.

A couple of years ago I was featured in a *Wall Street Journal* article about "humor in the workplace." It was a very positive article and one which painted a nice picture of the company I was working for which, incidentally, employed about 65,000 people. I received almost no feedback at all and absolutely none from any significant manager.

I remember seeing a video in the 1980s that illustrated how important feedback was by showing a person bowling. Immediate feedback came in the form of seeing how many pins went down. A curtain was then placed in the alley so the bowler could not see how many pins were hit. That is more like the normal state of feedback in most organizations.

"Metooism"—
Everyone is Doing it, So it Must be OK

How often have you driven 15 miles per hour over the speed limit and felt that it was OK because everyone else was doing it? There is a powerful force at work here called the "group norm." I believe that many things we do at work are done just because everyone else is doing it. Much too often, we define our directions based upon perceived truths. If we hear someone talking about another company that's doing benchmarking, we think, "That must be good—*they're* doing it."

In business, we are much too used to being followers rather than leaders. Too much of our energy is wasted latching onto things that are popular at the present time rather than things that are sensible. We don't question their true value. Large organizations seem to be most susceptible to "metooism" and they are often so slow that they miss any opportunity of applying the concepts while they are fresh. Smaller companies often provide leadership and momentum carrying out programs, many of which are valuable in the beginning. But, by the time the big companies get around to them, it's too late to reap the advantage of early implementation.

The areas of work teams and empowerment provide a good example. Small companies, and small geographically-separate units of larger ones, were able to gain competitive advantage by developing small-team environments and empowering people at lower levels of their companies. As more and more stories came out about the success of these endeavors, large companies said, "We need to do that too." Unfortunately, most companies that got on the bandwagon found that their organizational infrastructures were just not suited to this new way of life. Empowerment may work well for one company because its environment really believes in people. But for other companies, a huge cultural shift may be necessary before a program like this has any chance whatsoever. Twenty years ago I was involved in some intensive efforts to launch work teams at a major company. Despite some hard work on the part of many dedicated people, we were not very successful. They lacked an organizational culture that could accept this new way of designing work. While a few forward-looking internal consultants were trying to move the company ahead with contemporary work systems, most of the management and human relations people were still back in the dark ages.

Paternalistic and Caring Environments

There is a difference between being good to people and caring about them. Some large companies have a history of being paternalistic to their employees. They assume that, to motivate people, you must give them external rewards. This usually manifests itself in a series of programs that focus on keeping people happy. People are often happy on the outside but, down deep, are not satisfied.

I have talked with dozens of people from organizations that were depicted as "people oriented" only to hear that, from *their* perspective, the company couldn't care less about their people. This often comes to light when a company is experiencing difficult economic times and quickly turns away from its people. The answer to economic hard times always seems to be eliminating people (a cost burden) rather than energizing people (an asset to the business).

Truly caring environments in business can only occur when we realize the importance of relationships built upon genuine caring. When people care about each other it is hard *not* to care about the future of the organization.

Thought Provokers on Miscellaneous Irreverence

1. Do the activities within your company suggest an orientation to external or internal motivation?

2. Are there programs or activities that may be eroding long-term, healthy work relationships? What can you do about them?

3. Is there a caring environment within your organization?

4. Are there any signs of "not invented here" thinking within teams or individuals? If NIH is present, how is it manifesting itself and what can you do about it?

5. Spend some time observing the dynamics within your organization from a third-party perspective. What do you notice? How are these dynamics interfering with break-through change?

Chapter 7

Creativity at Work

The Hidden Resource

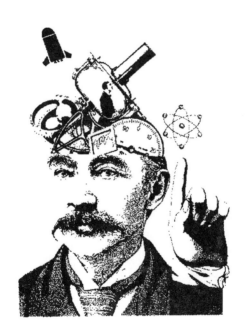

"It's always fun to do the impossible, because that's where there is less competition."—Walt Disney

Creativity at Work—the Impossible Dream

I am absolutely convinced that remarkable things can happen if businesses *really* create environments in which people can let loose their pent-up creative potential.

I'd be willing to bet that your organization has proclaimed that it values creativity. You know, those statements that come down from the mountain and proclaim how much management values its people and how much they believe in teamwork, trust, empowerment, creativity and all the other motherhood and apple pie things. Creativity is something organization managers say they want. Yet, where the rubber hits the road, most organizations stifle creativity.

I am convinced that creative people are looked at more often as a danger than as an asset. David Barry, in *Claw Your Way to the Top of the Organization*, suggests that business leaders must keep their subordinates happy, productive, hopeful and, above all, subordinate. He suggests a two-step process: making them think you are their friend, and getting rid of them if they start coming up with ideas. Remember the old saying: A subordinate capable of thinking up an idea is a subordinate capable of realizing that there is no particular reason he or she should be a subordinate, especially *your* subordinate. Creativity always involves risk, and there are very few companies I know of that reward risk. For the most part, *safe* behavior is rewarded. Even organizations that claim to encourage risk taking usually reward safe behavior.

I have seen some almost comical use of creative techniques such as brainstorming. Typical brainstorming consists of waiting for someone to come up with an idea. This is followed by long arguments as to why it won't work.

Other brainstorming sessions are tightly controlled to produce the maximum number of ideas. Negativism is banned. No one ever questions the guidelines for brainstorming that have been around for years. But we need to question why one of the objectives should be to generate as many ideas as possible.

The fact is that many brainstorming sessions that produce enormous numbers of ideas are often followed by meetings to determine why they can't be done. Or, as is more often the case, they are followed by nothing. In other words, no one knows what to do with all these ideas, so they sit on someone's desk until someone else suggests having another brainstorming session. You might just as well generate creative ideas and feed them directly into a shredder. Someone once said, "A problem well stated is a problem half solved." We should spend more time stating the problem clearly, and less time listing ideas about something ill defined.

There are several "centers of knowledge" in this country that purport to teach creativity. Each of these has its own process which it follows religiously. I find it interesting that these creativity gurus have such a difficult time breaking out of their own paradigms. Beware of the creativity consultant who comes to you with only one solution.

Brain Tickling and Brainstorming

We all have a tremendous cache of ideas lurking in our heads. But, we need to get them out into the open where we can work on them. There are hundreds of techniques that can help release those ideas. I refer to these techniques as "brain ticklers" and their objective is to help you to stretch your thinking. The techniques include viewpoint shifts, excursions, and metaphors.

Viewpoint shifts ask you to become someone, or something, you are not and to look at an opportunity or problem from that new viewpoint. Putting on different hats, thinking like your favorite hero, or becoming an object that is part of your problem statement are a few ways of mentally carrying out these shifts in perspective. Excursions are ways of getting far enough away from what you are working on so that you can find some interesting material that will provide creative connections. These can be word excursions, fantasy trips, catalog browsing, picture excursions or any number of other techniques to take creative people to places they have never been. Excursions are designed to make the familiar a little less familiar (or perhaps even strange) to help the mind stretch to new possibilities.

Metaphors allow us to identify and discuss our problem or opportunity in terms of something not normally associated with it. For example, if we want to identify some creative ways to enhance an organization, we might find the creativity enhanced by discussing what an organization has in common with an iceberg or an orchestra. Stories and myths provide terrific starting points for the use of metaphors.

Brain tickling requires a process consultant who is skilled in the creative techniques for helping you stretch outside your comfort zone.

Staying in the Comfort Zone

Everyone has three challenge zones: comfort, stretch, and breaking. In the comfort zone people take no risks, do what they are told, and stay out of trouble. In the stretch zone people question conventional wisdom, take risks, play with new and creative ideas, and look at things in very different ways.

In the breaking zone you jump to something that seems to be totally impossible. For example, I think I will enter the Olympics this summer as a champion high jumper.

Pretend for a moment that you are an elastic band. At what point do you feel your best? When you are relaxed and sagging? When you are stretched to the breaking point? The most satisfying state for you should be when you are experiencing a firm, challenging stretch. Keep that band in mind the next time you are feeling over, or under, challenged.

What percentage of people in work do you feel are in each of these categories? I think you will agree with me that nearly everyone is in the comfort zone. To achieve results from physical exercise you need to carry it to the point where you can't go any farther. Muscle develops only when you bring it well into the stretch zone. That's the secret that helped launch Nautilus. People, and businesses, develop in the same way. Our brain operates much the same as our muscles. The more you develop your mental capacities through stretching, the more becomes available to you. If most people are in the comfort zone, where is the organization's creative growth? Are people mentally dying at work? What are the implications of a work environment that really stretches people? People, like rubber bands, when stretched never go back to their original position. Rubber bands that are never touched eventually shrivel and disintegrate. When an old band is stretched it breaks. People who are continually pushed into their stretch zone will be continually moving toward challenging the impossible.

Isn't it time to push people out of their comfort zones?

The Nature of Creativity and Breakthrough

In creativity workshops I ask the question: "What were you doing when you last had a great idea?" What would your answer to this question be? The most common answers include driving the car, brushing my teeth, taking a shower, and sleeping. I have never had anyone say that they got a great idea in a meeting or while sitting at their desk. Perhaps we need to supply more toothbrushes, showers, and couches in the workplace. Here are a few of the characteristics of creativity. How does your organization integrate these into the work environment?

- **Breakthrough often comes from exploring outside your box**.

If, for example, you are a mechanical engineer looking for a breakthrough, you may want to look outside the engineering box. Perhaps art, politics, music, or some other seemingly unrelated field contains the answer you are looking for. You can study other fields or ask people in these areas for possible metaphors. Kodachrome was invented by two musicians. An undertaker invented the automatic telephone dialing system. And, as I mentioned earlier, an actuary designed a new, possibly revolutionary, tennis racquet handle. If you are involving a group in an ideation process, you should have a diverse group that includes people well outside the existing box in which you would normally look for an answer. Your creativity and the collective creativity of your group are likely to be strongly enhanced by doing some study outside your normal field.

It is interesting to note that many organizations allow their associates paid education and development only in fields directly related to their work. The 3M company is a notable exception. This is a paradigm that needs to be shifted. I believe that learning that takes place outside one's normal boundaries creates the most exciting idea springboards. In other words, that basket weaving course you always joked about may not be a bad idea after all.

• Breakthrough tends to come when you least expect it—often after incubation.

Michael Ray in his book, *Creativity in Business*, suggests that a law of creativity should be, "If at first you don't succeed, give up." Ideas need time to incubate. Often the best thing to do is to file your problems in the three-pound incubation machine you carry around with you between your ears while waiting for an AHA! to occur. One of the blockages to creativity in the workplace is our need for immediate answers and our inability to take time for proper incubation of ideas.

• Breakthrough frequently results from stretching the mind to the absurd and then moving back to reality.

I recently saw a couple of cartoons that showed two new ideas for a diet. Just what we need, huh? One was called the "All you can suck through a 50-foot hose diet" and the other was the "All you can eat through a colander diet." These sound rather absurd but, if you spend a little time bringing the essence of these solutions back to reality, some new possibilities could emerge. Many of the techniques I use in my "brain tickling" sessions are those which stretch our thinking into the absurd, then "float" it back to reality.

• Breakthrough often comes from tapping a fresh mind, like that of a child.

I was just reading about a 10-year-old girl who invented a Christmas tree ornament called a "guardian angel." She was worried about the danger of the Christmas tree catching fire and noticed the angel at the top of her tree. A combination of this ornament and a smoke detector created a wonderful new product. If all else fails, ask some kids and you may be pleasantly surprised.

• Many breakthroughs are amazing in their simplicity.

We tend to think of breakthroughs as being complex solutions. Einstein once said, "Make it as simple as possible but no more." If we train ourselves to look at simplicity we will open up tremendous possibilities. Some of our most creative ideas come when you factor a problem or opportunity to its essence. Perhaps the reason why people who are not a part of the problem can contribute creative ideas has something to do with the fact that they haven't yet raised their thinking to a level of complexity that limits them.

• Breakthrough is possible and necessary in all aspects of business and life.

The importance of breakthrough seems to be recognized only in a few areas such as new products, scientific discovery, marketing, and advertising. Achieving creative breakthrough in areas such as human relations, finance, and publications is often ignored. As a result, these are wonderful areas for creative thinking processes. As a last resort, some companies may need to creatively achieve some accounting breakthroughs.

Blockages to Creativity

For us to better understand how to bring out people's latent creativity, it is important to understand that all the creativity we need resides in our associates but is blocked by a number of obstacles. Studies repeatedly show that there is enormous creativity in children—which should make us ask: "Where does it all go?" Obviously the creative capacity of children is chipped away by adults until there isn't much left. But that's really not true—it's still there, it's just smothered by other things. Roger von Oech says, "Children start school as question marks and leave as periods." The late Harry Chapin wrote a song called, "Flowers are Red" which tells the story of a little boy who began his first day of school crayoning colors all over his paper. When the teacher asked what he was doing, he said he was drawing flowers. The teacher told him that it wasn't the right time to be drawing flowers—and that flowers were supposed to be red and green. The chorus throughout the song is:

> Flowers are red, green leaves are green. There's no need to see flowers any other way than the way they always have been seen.

The little boy said, "There are so many colors in the rainbow, so many colors in the morning sun. So many colors in a flower and I see every one." As you can probably guess, the teacher finally convinced the little boy that there was only one way to draw flowers and that he must do it the "right" way. He later went to another school where his new teacher tried to convince him that "painting should be fun and there are so many colors in a flower," But the little boy had learned to do things the "right" way and could only paint his flowers in neat rows of green and red. How often is this story acted out within our schools today? What effect does it have on a learning organization? How are you limited by what you learned long ago was "right"?

We can't blame all stilted thinking on the schools because parents usually get the first shot. As parents we seem to think our job is to tell our kids the one best way to do everything. In our own minds we have defined the "right" way and that is what our children will do. Their schooling and their first jobs usually carry this tradition on to the point that, by the time a child is a young adult, there is little incentive to stretch beyond the comfort zone. What are the things that block your creativity?

Psychological constraints are powerful areas of blockage. One is our normal tendency, or preference, for the orderly and predictable and our intolerance for the unknown and ambiguous. Another is our need for high achievement and quick results which doesn't allow time for ideas to incubate. Our tendency to value "that which is" rather "that which is possible" blocks us from seeing beyond things that are easy to grasp because they are not much different from what we now have.

Perhaps the most powerful psychological block to creativity is our fear of failure. This fear is much more powerful than most of us will admit. In organizations, fear of failure can drive the entire thinking process! Cultural constraints limit the creativity of people at work. The values and beliefs that we acquire from parents, teachers, bosses, and peers can guide us but they can also block us from thinking creatively. High value is often placed on reason, logic, numbers, practicality, and rightness. Low value is often placed on the things that bring out creativity: playfulness, fantasy, reflection, and humor.

Environmental constraints are both physical and social. Most workplace environments provide little stimulation to the mind. Some of the most creative sessions I have done with groups were done by getting out of the workplace. Interesting conference centers, boats, parks, museums and, of course, humor rooms (see chapter 8) help to bring out new thinking. The social environment of the workplace is often one that does not reward creative thinking. I don't believe I've ever seen a performance appraisal process that includes a look at how well a candidate has done in areas that stimulate creativity (such as making mistakes, taking risks, and having fun).

The last in this series of creativity blocks is thinking-process constraints. We tend to think either in verbal, mathematical, or visual terms. Our ability to be creative is limited when we make the wrong choice. Let me illustrate with a couple of problems for you:

I wrap a steel band around the earth so that it just touches the surface (assume a smooth surface). I then walk up to it, cut it, and add a 40-foot section. I re-wrap it around the Earth (which is a distance of about 25,000 miles) so that it is an equal distance at all points from the smooth surface of the Earth and my question to you is: what is the distance between Earth and the band? Is it enough for an ant to walk under or enough for an aunt to walk under? (If you are from Boston, it is hard to tell the difference between the two.) Chances are that you are trying to visualize this and it is difficult to see whether adding 40 feet to a 25,000-mile distance will have any impact at all. If you had decided to work it out mathematically you would use a very simple equation and find there is enough distance for your aunt to walk under it—if, of course she is about five feet eight inches tall.

Other process constraints include what we call "functional fixedness." It is the tendency to get stuck on what objects are *supposed* to do. We have fixed in our minds what a hammer, a chair, dental floss, etc., are supposed to do and resist imagining their being used for drastically different things. We also tend to get stuck in habitual ways of visualizing things. Betty Edwards, in her book, *Drawing on the Right Side of the Brain*, gives a series of wonderful demonstrations that show how we can overcome our inability to draw by upsetting our habits of visualizing. One example is to try to sketch something from an existing picture that we are familiar with. If you are not satisfied with the results, try to sketch it from the upside-down picture and see the differences. This simple change gets us away from our habitual way of visualizing what we are drawing, and the results can be quite amazing.

Creating an Environment for Creativity in the Workplace

What are the characteristics of a work environment that stimulate creativity? Arthur B. Van Gundy from the University of Oklahoma suggests that we should consider this from three positions:

1. Each individual's internal environment.
2. The quality of interpersonal relationships within groups or teams.
3. The environment that surrounds the group.

The individual's internal environment recognizes that each person has a different measure of the characteristics for being creative. These characteristics include:

- Curiosity
- Ability to defer judgment
- Optimism
- Humor
- Openness to others' ideas
- Persistence
- Self confidence
- Tolerance for ambiguity
- Spontaneity or impulsiveness
- Ability to use imagery
- Ability to concentrate on a problem

The quality of interpersonal relationships in work groups and teams is also a key source for opening (or closing) the capacity for creativity. Included here are:

- Interpersonal trust

- Acceptance of deviant behaviors and ideas
- Willingness for (and quality of) listening
- Spirit of cooperation
- Encouragement for expression of ideas
- Open confrontation of conflicts
- Friendliness toward one another
- Respect for each other's feelings
- Lack of defensiveness
- Inclusion of all group members

And, finally, we need to look at the environment that surrounds the individuals and groups in terms of how it allows for creativity to take place. Characteristics to consider here include:

- Freedom for trying new ways
- Low level of supervision
- Delegated responsibility
- Encouragement of participation
- Challenging work goals
- Necessary resources provided
- Divergent ideas accepted
- Open expression encouraged
- Time provided for creative efforts
- Confidence exhibited in people
- Interaction with outside resources encouraged
- Timely feedback required

Van Gundy provides a questionnaire in his book, *Managing Group Creativity*, to help assess the current state of these characteristics in your organization. Ask yourself how your organization stacks up regarding all of these characteristics. For those that you are weak in, explore how to improve. If there are significant problems in the creative environment, which of the three areas are the major source of these problems. What can you do to turn this around? Another viewpoint comes from the Creative Education Foundation in Buffalo, N.Y., which suggests the following ten traits of the creative climate in an organization. These are based on the work of Goran Ekvall in Sweden. As we explore these traits ask yourself how your own organization's environment measures against them and what you might do to enhance them in your own situation.

1. **Challenge:** The emotional involvement of the members of the organization in its operations and goals.

A high-challenge climate exists when people experience joy and meaningfulness in their jobs, and therefore, invest much energy. Low challenge produces feelings of alienation and indifference; the common sentiment and attitude is apathy and lack of interest for the job and the organization. Recall the previous discussion on being in the comfort zone. Creativity and breakthrough never come from the comfort zone.

2. **Freedom:** The independence in behavior exerted by the people in the organization.

In a climate with much of this kind of freedom, people are making contacts to give and receive information and to discuss problems and alternatives. They plan and take initiatives of different kinds and they make decisions. The opposite of this climate would include people who are passive, rule-fixed, and anxious to stay inside their frames and established boundaries.

3. **Idea Support:** The ways new ideas are treated.

In a supportive climate, ideas and suggestions are received in an attentive and kind way by bosses and peers. People listen to each other and encourage initiatives. Possibilities for trying out new ideas are created. The atmosphere is constructive and positive. When idea support is low you hear "no" and "yeah-but" a lot. Every suggestion is immediately put down by a counter-argument. Fault-finding and obstacle-raising are the usual styles of responding to ideas. What typically happens in your organization when new ideas are expressed?

4. **Trust and Openness:** The emotional safety in relationships. When there is a strong level of trust, everyone in the organization dares to put forward ideas and opinions. Initiatives can be taken without fear of reprisal and ridicule. The communication is open and straightforward. Where trust is missing, people are suspicious of each other and are afraid of being exploited and robbed of their good ideas.

5. **Dynamism and Liveliness**: The eventfulness of life in the organization.

In highly dynamic situations, new things are happening all the time and alternations between ways of thinking about and handling issues often occur. There is a kind of psychological turbulence which is described by people in those organizations as "full speed," "go," "breakneck," and the like. The opposite situation could be compared to a slow jog-trot with no surprises. There are no new projects; no different plans. Everything goes its usual way.

6. **Playfulness and Humor:** The spontaneity and ease that is displayed.

A relaxed atmosphere with jokes and laughter characterizes the organization which is high in this dimension. The opposite climate is characterized by gravity and seriousness. The atmosphere is stiff, gloomy and cumbrous. Jokes and laughter are regarded as improper. In the next chapter we'll take an exclusive look at the role of humor.

7. **Debates:** The occurrence of encounters and clashes between viewpoints, ideas, and differing experiences, and knowledge.

In a debating organization, many voices are heard and people are keen on putting their ideas forward. Where debates are missing, people follow authoritarian patterns without question. Debates should take place through dialogue in which all parties are able to express their feelings openly.

8. **Conflicts:** The presence of personal and emotional tensions in the organization.

When the level of conflict is high, groups and individuals dislike each other and the climate can be characterized as "warfare." Plots and traps are usual elements in the life of the organization. There is gossip and slander going on. In the opposite case, people behave in a more mature manner: they have psychological insight and control of impulses.

9. **Risk Taking:** The tolerance of uncertainty exposed in the organization.

In the high-risk-taking case, decisions and actions are prompt and rapid, arising opportunities are taken, and trying is preferred to detailed investigation and analysis. In a risk-avoiding climate there is a cautious, hesitant mentality. People try to be on the "safe side." They decide to "sleep on the matter." They set up committees and they cover themselves in many ways before making a decision.

10. **Idea Time:** The amount of time people can use for elaborating new ideas.

In an idea-time situation, the possibilities exist to discuss and test impulses and fresh suggestions that are not planned or included in the task assignment. People tend to use these possibilities. In the reverse case, every minute is booked and specified. The time pressure makes thinking outside the instructions and planned routines impossible.

How does your organization stack up against these creative climate dimensions?

Work: 5 Days of Pain
for a 2-Day Reward

Somewhere along the line the assumption was formed that work should be a painful experience. It does not seem right to pay people for having fun. "Fun work" is an oxymoron like "friendly artillery" or "professional wrestling." The words, "serious fun" also don't go together by most people's standards. And yet, people can perform tasks that they enjoy much better than those they don't. When people are having fun and enjoying their activities they are usually doing a great job. Why can't work be that way? If so many people are disgruntled about their jobs could humor in the workplace help them to be gruntled?

Provocative Questions About Creativity in the Workplace

1. How many of the creative climate dimensions can be found in your workplace? How do you rate yourself regarding these dimensions?

2. Name some specific shortcomings that detract from the ability of your organization to be creative.

3. How can you bring about a change in these dimensions?

4. Are there some good opportunities for brain tickling sessions in your organization? Where, specifically?

5. Name some specific areas that could use creative thinking processes in your company.

Chapter 8

The Positive Impact of Humor in the Workplace

Your Fun Bone's Connected To Your Work
Bone

"You are only young once—but you can be
immature all of your life."—anonymous

Humor in the Workplace— You've Got to be Kidding

I can honestly say that humor can have a wonderful effect on people at work. Facilitating hundreds of groups in creative-thinking processes has convinced me that, when people are able to be humorous, creativity follows. And I have seen cases where humor has had a dramatic and positive effect on the dynamics of the workplace, from helping people get along with each other to helping them cope with change. I studied the effects of positive humor on work a few years ago and believe I have discovered one of the least used resources in the workplace. It is also one of the most misunderstood connections because so many people are convinced that work is serious business and has no room for humor.

But humor, used in the right way, can be one of the most powerful resources available to help people be effective in their work.

Stated another way, humor can help you achieve "funtastic" results in your work.

Someday We'll all Laugh at This

Often when I discuss with managers the possibility of humor as a valuable resource, I get a funny look along with comments like these:

"That sounds interesting. When things improve around here we'll have to try that."

"I'd be interested in knowing more about this after we get these problems behind us."

"Someday we'll laugh about all this."

The question is: "Why wait?" Humor and laughter can help you over the rough spots.

Paul Hawken in his 1987 book published by Fireside, *Growing a Business*, says, "I don't believe there is a business in America that would not benefit from loosening up and having fun with its customers." He uses the analogy of coal miners bringing birds into the shafts for early warnings of danger and says, "Laughter and good humor are the canaries of the mine of commerce. When the laughter dies, its an early warning that life is ebbing from the enterprise."

Work and Fun—The Ultimate Oxymoron

Over the years I've worked with many people. My favorites were those who found time each day to tell a joke or two, engage in humorous small talk, and digress occasionally from the serious work at hand What I didn't recognize at that time was that this humor was rarely "connected" to the work. It was simply time out from work to be humorous.

The assumption about the relationship between humor and work was the same then as, in most cases, it is now. Humor, if allowed to take place at all, is time out from the seriousness of work. This feeling is even stronger during periods of economic downturn when obsession with solemnity in work can be overbearing. Another way of putting it is that humor and seriousness are assumed to be a "zero sum game." Work is supposed to be painful and pain is not supposed to be enjoyed. I am serious about my work and feel others should be too. But who ever said it had to be a solemn, painful experience? If you believe nothing else, believe this:

Humor can have a powerful and positive effect on the business of work and can be entwined effectively in our everyday work life in a way that enhances both our feelings about work and the quality of our output. Work doesn't have to be five days of pain for which we get a two-day reward. Imagine a scenario that involves people who really enjoy their work, one in which TGIM (Thank God It's Monday!) is a common statement. Effective use of positive humor at work may just help us realize this scenario but the relationship between humor and work needs to undergo a shift. The idea is to create a situation in which humor is used positively to enhance work and is accepted as a powerful resource. We need to nurture this relationship between humor and work over the long term.

Few managers recognize humor as a resource. And those who do only accept humor as a temporary respite from the seriousness of work. "Let's give them a humor break now and then." "We'll bring in a humor consultant to entertain them for a while." Humor consultants love this; it keeps them busy. But these approaches will not change the relationship between humor and work. They will only provide temporary relief from the pain.

Effective use of humor involves building the ability of individuals so they can consistently use their humor, along with their other skills, to increase the effectiveness of everything they do. I told a friend of mine that I was going to explore the connection between humor and work to see if I could come up with some ways to help people use humor productively. His response surprised me until I realized how correct he was. He said, "Don't do too good a job at it because they might start a humor program, and that will surely kill it."

And he was right, as soon as you label something as a "program" you have given it the kiss of death. We don't need a humor program, we need a paradigm shift in how we think about the humor and work. People need to learn how to use their humor potential to help them in their work. But most people don't think they are very humorous.

I look at being humorous and creative as having similar traits. Most people don't think they are creative either but they often are. A good place to begin is to create more openness so people can use humor in work situations without fear of ridicule. And, while you are at it, be more open to creativity as well. The two will build on each other.

Positive and Negative Humor

Humor can be misused. I want to make sure you understand that I am talking about the use of humor that supports and strengthens people at work. You have seen situations where humor was used to disguise angry or spiteful feelings or to cover up lack of competence or to circumvent issues that needed discussion. This kind of humor is negative, that is, it is nonproductive. If people feel pain as a result of the "joke," or if forward movement of the group is derailed, something needs work. Let's perpetuate the positive and negate the negative.

Positive humor enhances the relationships of people at work. It comes from a position of caring about others. People who really care about each other will rarely use humor in a negative way. When positive humor is used, people are drawn closer together. Negative humor, on the other hand, tends to victimize people and harm relationships by masking real feelings. It comes from a position of weakness or from a desperate attempt to "look good"—often at the expense of making someone else look bad. It frequently comes across as contrived.

Why is Humor so Important
in the Workplace?

- It can reduce stress and result in healthier employees because of the close connection between humor and physical and mental health. People who are able to use humor as a natural resource in their work are happier and healthier.

- It can stimulate the creative potential in people. The resulting creative thinking opens up new possibilities for the future of the organization.

- It can help build strong relationships between people. Strong teams come from these relationships and humor is one of building blocks of these teams.

- It can improve the ability to effectively communicate by making conversation more exciting and rewarding.

- It can dramatically improve training. I remember clearly those training activities that were fun. I quickly forgot the dull ones.

- It can help people cope with change. And don't we all need help here?

Humor and Health in the Workplace

The positive effect of humor on people's health has been realized intuitively for a long time. But, over the past few years, there has been growing interest to explore this more deeply. Norman Cousins, formerly editor of the *Saturday Review,* wrote a book in 1979 called *The Anatomy of an Illness.* He relates his experience of using humor to laugh himself back from a disease which had been diagnosed as terminal. His story was so compelling that people began serious study of the connection between humor and health. At a recent World Future Society conference, Earl Bakken suggested, "For most of our health problems, all we really need is a physician to amuse us while our body recovers." There is a saying, "I laughed myself to death." I don't know of a single case of this, but I do know some people who have laughed themselves to "life."

A large body of evidence is accumulating that supports the theory that humor has a positive effect on health and well being. If positive humor in the workplace results in healthier people to do the work, shouldn't we be interested in humor's connection to the physical and mental health of our most important resource?

Let me give you a very quick, non-technical explanation of what happens when you enjoy a good laugh. At first there is an elevation of your blood pressure, breathing, and heart rate. When you stop laughing these drop quickly and the result is a "high" feeling. There is also a release of endorphins, the body's natural opiates. I am not sure what these characters really are but I like to picture them as in-body Pac Men that wander around eating up anything that shouldn't be there. (I told you this would be non-technical.) It has been suggested that laughter is a form of "internal jogging." It causes your internal organs to get to know each other a little better. Some say that laughter also has a great laxative effect, which would explain why joke books are often found in bathrooms. Norman Cousins states in *The Anatomy of an Illness*, "I never knew a person possessed by the gift of hearty laughter to be burdened by constipation."

Now that I have given you indisputable scientific evidence that humor affects our physical well being, what about our mental health? I am sure you can cite many occasions where humor has pulled you out of the mental doldrums. When people at work are depressed, a situation not all that uncommon these days, someone needs to start them on an upward mental spiral. I can't think of anything better than positive humor—and it's cheaper and more effective than therapy. People who feel good about themselves and their situation perform better. It's that simple.

Humor and Creativity in the Workplace

When was the last time you had a great idea in a dull situation? I have attended some incredibly dull meetings (*most* of them) and their results were usually equally as dull. It's been said that a meeting is an event where minutes are kept and hours are lost. You can often measure the creative output of a meeting by the laughter and lightness of it. I am not suggesting that you turn all your activities into mini versions of *Monty Python's Flying Circus*. Remember, work and humor can have a symbiotic relationship just like those small birds that hang around on the backs of rhinoceroses. Each helps the other.

The connection between humor and creativity is often called the Ha-Ha/Aha connection. (In Japan it is the Ha-Ha/Aha/Ah-So connection.) Humor and creativity are closely connected because they have similar characteristics:

- Humor and creativity spring from similar techniques. Techniques that help people think creatively include: putting unlike things together, playing with incongruities, metaphors, excursions, freewheeling, and re-framing. These also help people create humor.

- Humor and creativity are both resources that many people have convinced themselves they don't have. Most people will tell you they are neither creative or humorous. Everyone has the potential for both but their use is often blocked.

- Both humor and creativity are risky. Creativity is defined as going somewhere you haven't been before. As Frank Lloyd Wright once said, "If the roof doesn't leak, the architect probably hasn't been very creative." In some organizations, suggesting that work should be fun can be risky.

- Both humor and creativity tend to come about logically and unexpectedly. As someone once said, "An invention is like the punch line of a joke—completely logical and completely unexpected."

- The traits of humorous people and creative people are pretty much the same. Both are right brain oriented, tend to be spontaneous, and tend to march to the beat of a different drummer.

- Both humor and creativity are summoned more easily when you are feeling good about yourself. They are more attitude oriented than skill oriented.

- Humor and creativity both make frequent passes from fantasy to reality.

A chapter in *The Anatomy of an Illness* is entitled "Creativity and Longevity." It deals with the proposal that people who are continually stretching their creativity tend to live longer. We've have already seen that people who exercise their humor live longer. You now have two methods for living longer and that should be worth the price of this book.

Humor and Healthy Relationships in the Workplace

Pianist and humorist Victor Borge once said, "Humor is the shortest distance between two people." When you think about it, effective work is really a matter of creating effective conversations between people. Good communication comes from a complex set of relationships, and humor can be a powerful enhancement. Unfortunately it can also be used destructively, so let me remind you that I am focusing on positive humor, the humor that comes from caring about others. You have seen situations in which humor has been used to cover up incompetence or real feeling about people.

Humor which comes from a caring person, however, will nearly always be used in a way that brings people closer together. I learned a long time ago that people help others who display a sense of humor. In one situation, our group's secretary was trying to improve her response to work requests and asked that we write down when we needed our work back. Of course, most said, "ASAP" or indicated a specific date. On one document that I really wanted quickly but couldn't give a good reason for I wrote, "Sometime before the end of time." To my surprise, this went right to the top and I had it within hours. The lesson here is that humor can help you get action.

There are a couple of areas where humor has some interesting connections. The first is conflict resolution. The premise is: if I am laughing with someone, I can't fight with him. There is an almost magical attraction that occurs between people who are enjoying a humorous moment so it makes sense that humor can help to resolve conflicts. A while back the police in an upstate New York town were experimenting with the use of humor. When responding to domestic disputes, they would send two officers to the scene, one dressed normally and the other dressed as Bugs Bunny. When the door was answered, Bugs would say, "What's up Doc," walk into the house and raid the refrigerator. John Morreal, a Professor at Rochester Institute of Technology, defines humor as "a pleasant incongruity", and costumed cops fit that description. Since it is impossible to enjoy the laughter of a pleasant incongruity and fight at the same time, the conflict gives way to the humor of the situation.

The other area that I believe is under explored is the connection between humor and sales. The premise is: if I can get someone laughing with me, I can sell them anything. Commercials using humor are consistently the highest rated. Salespeople who are able to create a good rapport with their clients using humor are consistently the most effective.

I hope I have convinced you that humor can create better relationships in the workplace. Begin your next meeting with a few minutes designed to loosen things up and just watch the results.

Humor and Your Ability to Communicate Effectively

As I think about the many speakers I have heard and seen, it is clear to me that the most memorable were those who had just the right touch of humor in their presentation, but not so much that their messages were disguised. It is easy to forget the dull speakers. It is also easy to forget the humorous ones who had no message. The right amount of humor connected to a clear message ensures that the message is remembered too.

When communication is taking place, in a group or one-on-one, humor can make listeners more receptive to what you have to say. Humor opens up the listening and accepting part of the communication process. We are attracted to people who communicate in a lighthearted but purposeful way. Humor is to communicating as warm-up stretching is to exercise. It makes your listening muscles ready to accept new information without hurting themselves.

Humor in your Training

The importance of humor in the creation of effective communication suggests its importance in training. Training sessions that include good doses of laughter really open up the learning channels. Training without humor can shut down the brain and so many training programs these days have the same effect as sleeping pills. There is absolutely no reason why learning can't be fun. People tend to learn and remember things which tickled their funny bones.

Humor and Coping With Change and Other Disasters

Years ago, large businesses were stable. Somewhere along the line this changed, and I believe the change is permanent. Stability will not be a common sight in the future. Since change is difficult for many people, we need to help them cope with it. Using positive humor can make the change a lot more palatable. Being in a humorous state of mind helps people see the bright side of things. As one company was laying off workers in yet another wave of "downsizing" someone circulated posters which spoofed a current movie, *Honey, I Shrunk the Kids*. As you may have guessed they said, "Honey, I Shrunk the Company." They actually made people feel a little better about what was happening.

Humor is one of the best resources you have to help you through the rough spots in your business and personal life. A few years ago, my wife was diagnosed as having ovarian can-

127

cer, a life-threatening disease. The ability of my family and me to draw upon our humor resources helped us to get through this. Fortunately, everything turned out well. Humor helped us get through it, but it also may have set up the conditions for a successful outcome. In the same time period, a car accident claimed the life of a close family member. Again, humor played a major role in helping us cope with this situation. I hope that these insights and illustrations are enough to convince you that humor in workplace is a valuable resource.

The Forms of Humor at Work

Humor comes in many shapes and sizes. Let's take a look at these categories and a few examples and discuss when they may be appropriate.

Jokes

Joel Goodman from the Humor Project has said that one of the great myths of humor is that, "all humor is in the form of jokes." If you are humorous, you are expected to tell jokes. I rarely use jokes because I can't remember them and I think many jokes are designed to take victims. Taking victims is not positive humor. I am not an anti-joke person, I just prefer other forms of humor.

Quotations and quips

Quotations are great learning tools and, those that are humorous, are even greater. The quotation, "Life is like being on a dog sled team. If you ain't the lead dog, the scenery never changes," is humorous but also may serve as an insightful analogy for discussion of a business situation. I'll let you fill in the details here. "For every vision, there is an equal and opposite revision" may help you to enter into a light, but serious, discussion of a visioning process. And "Teamwork is important. It provides other people for managers to shoot at" may help free up a discussion of the importance of teamwork.

Funny signs and slogans

At the airport in Rochester, New York, there is a shoeshine service that sports this sign: "If your shoes aren't becoming to you, then you should be coming to us." Now there's a place that someone can walk into and feel right at home. The sign contains an imbedded message: "We are fun to deal with and you'll enjoy the experience." A sign outside a beauty salon that says, "Ears pierced while you wait," will stop and make you think. And a sign outside a bakery that says, "Get your buns in here," just may convince you to.

Cartoons

Cartoons are terrific sources of levity and creativity for meetings, presentations and other occasions but should be carefully chosen so they connect well with the situation. I find it useful to keep a file of cartoons to draw from for meetings and going through them always makes it worthwhile.

Analogies

Use analogies to help people think creatively. This process almost always brings out the humor in people. Why is organizational downsizing like liposuction? This question will produce lively, interesting, and humorous discussion and some new insights beyond that which would come from a normal question.

Outrageous statements and behavior

Real creativity rarely comes from normalcy. This form of humor allows you to get outside your normal comfort zone. The view is much different from there and you'll be able to make some creative connections. One of my favorite books is Tom Weller's, *Book of Stupid Questions* from Warner Books. It's full of questions such as:

- If you could change the order of the alphabet, what order would you put it in?
- What is your favorite internal organ?
- Do you have a favorite toe?
- Have you ever been a member of the opposite sex and how do you know you're not?
- Would you be willing to go to Hell if you could have the Gatorade concession?

A comedian that uses outrageous humor well is Steven Wright. A creative session held after listening to Wright's great outrageous stories and fantasies would be truly interesting. I sometimes personally prepare for creative sessions by doing something like driving backwards past a McDonalds drive up window, reminiscing with someone I've never met, or ordering swordfish ice cream from the local dairy bar.

Aikido

This is a verbal form of the martial art. If you are verbally attacked you have four options. You can fight back, run away, stand there and take it, or go with the flow. The aikido approach goes with the flow by sensing the specific characteristics of the attack and using them to neutralize it. This is best explained by an example which involves an obscene phone call. "I would like to take off your underwear," said the caller. An aikido response might be, "I didn't know you were wearing my underwear."

As you can see, this is a relatively gentle form of verbal martial art. It has the potential to resolve conflict in a way that neither party is hurt. Think of the possibilities in business.

How Might We Use Humor in the Workplace?

Here are a few ways you might use humor in your own work situation. I invite you to add your own ideas to this list.

☺ Take daily humor breaks. Real quality or creative thinking rarely comes when you force it. If you need a break, make it a humor break. Read a humorous book, listen to a comedian, do something really weird. Your time will be well spent.

☺ Keep a humor notebook. Somewhere in your file drawer or computer should be a collection of cartoons, jokes, funny observations and other items that you can draw on when needed. It's a great place to find humor to take to a meeting and a great place for a break.

☺ Watch for silly, incongruous activities. If you can't find any, make them up in your own mind.

☺ Display humorous things around you. Keeping light hearted items close to you helps to lighten you up when you need it. It also signals others that you are an easy person to work with.

☺ Laugh at yourself a lot. You are your own best source of humor and, if you begin taking yourself too seriously, you're in trouble.

☺ Make your writings humorous. You don't have to be a comedy writer to be able to insert some light hearted comments into your memos. People will begin to look forward to your next one.

☺ Smile at everyone. It continually amazes me how few people will look others directly in the face, smile, and say "Hello" while passing. I make it a point to do this and you should too. It will make you feel good, even though others may sometimes think you're a little strange and wonder what you're up to.

☺ Go to a toy store often. And when you go, try not to be so grown up. Remember, creativity often comes from bringing the "kid" back.

☺ Start all meetings on a humorous note. Serious meetings need humor all the more. The worst meetings I have seen usually are attended by people who are stressed out when they come, and more stressed out when they leave. Humor relieves the stress that blocks their effectiveness.

☺ Start a humor support group. Sooner or later you will want to share the strength of your humor with others. The first humor support group I formed was to explore the potential of humor to help internal consultants in their work. We called this, "The Society for Prevention of Cruelty to Those Who Have Fun at Work."

The Humor Room

One way to strengthen the relationship between humor and work is to create humor rooms. These rooms are places where people can go to find resources that will help them gain access to humor and creativity. Mike Vance, one of Disney's original creativity gurus, tells how he created a "Kitchen of the Mind" in his home. Humor rooms are basically kitchens of the mind located in the workplace. You can go there to get resources, relax, reduce stress, make creative connections, gain new insights, shift paradigms and raise your level of

132

thinking. If the area is large enough, it may serve as a place for group ideation sessions.

Remember, breakthrough occurs only when we get outside our normal thought process. An area that is able to change people's viewpoints can influence this process of transforming thought. A properly designed and orchestrated humor and creativity room can dramatically stimulate new thinking. Here are nine specific reasons for a humor and creativity room in the workplace:

1. The room provides a refuge in which people can hunt for creative connections. Normal work environments are typically emotionally sterile and devoid of "idea connections."

2. The room provides employees with new ideas for using positive humor to carry out their work more effectively.

3. It provides a place to go to help reduce job stress.

4. It is a terrific area for networking around humor and creativity at work, sharing ideas about how humor might be used in positive ways to make work more productive and enjoyable.

5. It serves as a development area for new ideas.

6. It is a place to go just to lighten up, smile for a while, and go back to work with a new perspective.

7. It is a great place for ideation and brain tickling sessions.

8. It shows that your company is willing to support creative thinking.

9. It is tangible evidence that senior managers can point to when they try to tell others what a wonderfully modern company they are running.

The humor room's environment should be significantly different from anything that people are used to. The idea is to get people out of their boxes, not to lock them in. If normal offices have overhead fluorescent lighting, the humor room should have lamps that create a home-like atmosphere. If the rest of the plant or office has posters on quality or pictures of the company's founder, the humor room should have cartoon posters and pictures of Groucho Marx, Bill Cosby, and Woody Allen. The furniture should be comfortable and differ from what people are used to in their workplace. Colors should be bright and varied. In short, when people walk into the room, they should say to themselves, "This is nice! Where am I?"

The humor rooms I have designed have had four distinct areas. A resource area contains a healthy supply of books, reports, videos, and tapes and a comfortable area for people to use. A large humor room should have an area for events, complete with the audio-visual equipment necessary to play videos and tapes along with everything necessary to carry out presentations, discussions, and "braintickling" sessions.

Next there is the "toy shop." This is where you will find most of the things that make this room different. Being in this area is like shopping through an Archie McPhee catalogue or gift shops that carry toys and amusing gimmicks that help people lighten up. Among the things you'll find there are stress reducing gadgets (we had a large Sadam Husein punching bag), yo-yos, Slinkys, rubber body parts, rubber chickens, and several hats and disguises. These things come in very handy when carrying out brain tickling sessions as triggers for new ideas.

And, of course, we must have a high tech area for those who are not comfortable in a room without a computer. There are many very good software programs that help people release their creativity and humor and, if your budget can stand it, these could be set up to help electronically facilitate brainstorming sessions.

Of course, just opening a humor room without any supporting activities won't be effective. You should plan to help people understand the value of humor and how it connects to their creative capability, health, and ability to communicate. Some creativity workshops would help. You'll need a schedule of events that add excitement to the room. Each day there might be a noontime showing of a video or other activity such as a comic or magician, or you could conduct an interactive humorous session of some nature. The videos should include *Candid Camera*, *Monty Python*, *Saturday Night Live*, bloopers, old-time movies and some current comedians like Bill Cosby, Robin Williams, George Burns, and others. It's important to have lots of variety.

Humor is one of the most powerful resources available to help people achieve new levels of work. To take advantage of it, you must understand that it is an integral part of the work, not just "time out" from it.

Thought Provokers About Humor In The Workplace

1. Is humor considered an asset in your workplace?

2. How is humor typically used in your experience?

3. What is the "face value" of people in your workplace? Are they usually smiling or frowning?

4. What would it take to bring positive humor into your organization?

5. What specific things can be done to integrate humor into your workplace?

Chapter 9

Dialogue and Focused Conversation in the Workplace

"When you talk, you can only say something you know. When you listen, you may learn what someone else knows."— anonymous

A Look at Conversations
in the Workplace

I have worked for years to understand and develop new ways to develop a base for more creative thinking in the workplace. Only recently have I realized the real importance of the dynamics of conversation. One thing is obvious to me— pretty much all work is done through conversations. And most of the conversations people at work engage in are non-productive. Meetings, where conversation should be produc-tive, are usually opinion swapping sessions in which nothing of value is accomplished. How many times have you left a meeting wondering:

What was that all about?

Just what am I supposed to be doing?

Did we agree or commit to anything?

If this rings true you're not alone. The next time you have an opportunity to sit in on a meeting as an observer, try this: Think of yourself as a fly on the wall and listen carefully to everything that is said. When one person says something, lis-ten carefully for the responses from others. Think about what is being said from the listener's point of view. What is moti-vating that person to respond? How many conversations are focusing on creating something new rather than reacting to something in the past? Do the responses indicate an under-standing of what was said? What are the hidden meanings in the statements?

I think you will find this to be an interesting learning ex-perience. You may end up wondering how anything ever gets accomplished. Conversations in the workplace, in or out of meetings, are rarely focused on making things happen. If we could somehow learn how to do a better job at this we would have a far better chance to create a breakthrough. Conversations consist of both speaking and listening, but listening is by far the most important—and the most overlooked.

Listening

Some people have two modes of conversation: talking and waiting to talk. Small wonder that we tend to have listening problems. People tend to listen through the maze of their own background conversations. You know, the conversations we have with ourselves in our thoughts. Our background conversations come from a rich history of everything that has been stored in our brain. So when people listen there is a lot going on in their heads. They are likely listening through a complex set of filters. These filters help them make sense of what is being said relative to *their own* perceptions. They may also create a change in the meaning intended by the sender. Here are a few of the directions that these background conversations might be taking us.

- While listening, we are planning how to explain or justify our position or come up with a good excuse. Some of us line up excuses to use in case they are needed.
- We may be planning ways to avoid being dominated.
- We may be plotting ways to reject a thought simply because it is coming from someone you don't respect. Do you really listen with empathy to a politician of the opposite party?

- We may be thinking "We can't possibly make a difference—so let's just get the conversation over with and get on to something else."
- We may be listening just to agree, or disagree, with what is being said.
- We may adding all sorts of personal meaning that the speaker never intended.
- We may be interpreting expressed opinions as facts or threats.
- We may be preoccupied with looking good and telling ourselves how to preserve our self-image (our ego) in this stressful situation.
- We may be concerned about emerging as a winner.
- We may be listening and trying to decide how to protect our beliefs.
- We may be carrying out the act of listening, but already have "the answer."
- We may be thinking about how to hide our real feelings.
- We may be thinking about how to get *our* view to prevail.
- We may be planning how to end the conversation.

Dialogue

Theoretical physicist David Bohm proposes a new way of listening to each other and hearing ideas without judgment. He calls this "dialogue." The *Utne Reader*, a contemporary magazine, has established "salons" which engage groups in dialogue around different subject areas and are currently reaching 13,000 people. Bohm suggests that normal discussion is like a Ping-Pong™ game in which people bat ideas back and forth in order to win. In Bohm's dialogue, there is no attempt to gain points, or to make your particular point prevail. People are not playing a game against each other, but *with* each other. Just think of the possibilities with this type of conversation.

The entire process of dialogue, according to Bohm, involves some shifts in thinking that may challenge many groups. Dialogues do not have agendas. That challenges our assumption that, to accomplish something, you must have a clear purpose. Along with an agenda for accomplishing a goal comes assumptions about what is useful, and that will be limiting. Dialogues don't have leaders and are not limited to small groups. The point of dialogue is not to come to an answer. It is to "soften up," to open up minds so they are able to look at all options. It is more concerned with finding meaning than with finding truth. In dialogue, we come to a meeting open to change instead of wanting to win. Think of the possibilities in your organization if people focus on being open to change rather than focusing on being right.

You can find outstanding examples of dialogue by watching the tribal councils in the movie, *Dances With Wolves*. I have used this model in many groups. To learn how to engage in dialogue, it is usually necessary to unlearn a few things.

- We think that winning is the point.
- We defend our current beliefs rather than learn something new.
- We perceive others' opinions as threats rather than opportunities to change our own thinking.
- We are conditioned to adversarial discussion.
- We tend to equate openness with naiveté and vulnerability.
- We find it difficult to tolerate the frustration of conflict without focus.
- We feel that, if we disagree, we must agree before disengaging.

Most of us are firmly trained in the ways of *discussion* and not *dialogue* and it will take some patience and frustration to feel comfortable with the process of dialogue. It's well worth the effort. Here are a few guidelines.

- Adopt an attitude of learning. If you consider every event as an opportunity to learn or to change the way you think, you are on the right track.
- Avoid non-negotiable positions. Dialogue never occurs between people who adopt the position: "That's the way it is."
- Be willing to suspend your assumptions.
- Embody a spirit of inquiry.
- Listen as an ally and act as a colleague.
- Focus on the content and meaning of the dialogue.
- Become an accomplished observer of yourself. It will be difficult to engage in dialogue if you can't observe yourself and honestly ask, "Am I successfully accomplishing the above."

We need a radical shift in how we engage in our conversations at work if we are to create breakthrough. This will not be easy. It has taken a long time to learn the present techniques of conversation with their many blocks to breakthrough.

Types of Conversations

Business conversations are purposeful. That is, we talk to each other to achieve a purpose. Though the purpose is not stated, the participants are usually aware of what the purpose of the conversation is. For example, we might talk to each other in order to prepare ourselves for a coming task. We are establishing the lay of the land. This kind of conversation is used to establish relationships between the players.

Another kind of conversation might be used to discuss possibilities. And a third might be used to discuss opportunities or goals we might pursue in the future. We might discuss the action we must take to achieve change or to reach goals. And we might also discuss how to deal with breakdowns, those things that prevent us from achieving our plans.

The following paragraphs explain these in greater detail.

Conversations for relationships

Any act of accomplishment requires that players establish a relationship. That sounds pretty simple but we often feel there is no need for a relationship in the workplace. In the colder climates of large organizations, some may even feel that relationships get in the way. Nevertheless, what we say or ask in a conversation is limited by the scope of the relationship.

Conversations that help to establish relationships require speaking and listening in a way that uses expressive speech. In expressive speech we reveal our position relative to the issue and the relationship. This is not "small talk" or social conversation or finding common interests. It is dialogue used to establish who the actors are and where they are coming from. It creates the right "chemistry" between people. And it depends a great deal upon the honesty that is expressed and on the opportunity at hand.

In conversations to establish relationships we need to communicate our state of psychological being. We need to let people know who we really are and what we really feel. People in many organizations don't feel safe doing this, which results in relationships that are not strong enough to support breakthrough change.

Conversation for possibility

Conversations for possibility are those which diverge to develop new thinking and ideas. When a relationship is established, conversations of possibility can begin to identify visions of breakthrough futures. Openness, creativity, and non-evaluation are critical components of this type of conversation. It is important to recognize that the conversation is about possibilities so the participants can relax their judgments. For many people, this is difficult since the words are modified as they pass through the listener's judgment filters. In conversations for possibility there is a distinct focus on the future. People must see themselves as standing in this future. A declaration of the future (such as, "We *will* have a man on the moon by 1970.") creates a real challenge that helps to make these conversations productive.

The speech involved in conversations for opportunity involves declarations and assertions. Declarations establish the possibility of something new. They bring forth the future simply by stating what will be and shift the relationship between present and future the moment they are spoken. Declarations must be stated by someone with recognized power and authority or they are not seen as meaningful. For me to declare a man and woman married means absolutely nothing. If a minister declares this it means a great deal. John F. Kennedy's declaration that Americans would put a man on the moon within ten years created the future and aimed the present toward that future.

Assertions are statements that something is true. When you make an assertion, you are expected to back it up with evidence. Assertions create energy and commitment to create something.

Conversations for opportunity

These conversations create the pathways between today and the vision of the future. There is a dangerous chasm between possibility and opportunity. History tells of many great ideas that have fallen into this chasm and never returned. People love to talk about possibilities. It's fun, invigorating, and exciting. When the conversation is about opportunity, it is necessary to be realistic. As you go from "fun" to "serious" there may be a loss of energy. I feel this is where many breakthrough projects peter out.

Conversations for action

These conversations involve getting a clear expression of the commitments necessary to accomplish breakthrough. It is here that possibility is translated into reality and promises and requests are needed. Intentions and ideas are converted into measurable results.

Action conversations use promises and requests. Requests bring forth action. Many people are reluctant to make requests and then wonder why nothing happens. Some people only request things that would happen anyway, fearing that asking for more would damage friendships. We want to look good, so we play it safe and the result is that we continue to produce mediocre results.

No requested action takes place without a promise. There must be a promise to match a request if there is to be a result. A promise says that you will produce the conditions of satisfaction specified by the requester in the future at an agreed time. It is an agreement of compliance.

Conversation for breakdown

Breakdowns are interruptions in the path that leads from now into the future. Having a strong declaration of the future will help you see breakdowns as opportunities. Breakthrough occurs when we creatively address breakdowns. Traditional emphasis avoids breakdowns. Breakthrough emphasis thrives on breakdowns because it recognizes that, if there were no breakdowns, there would probably be no breakthroughs either.

Thought Provokers on Dialogue and Conversation

1. Observe some listening habits (including your own) in a variety of work activities and carefully identify what's happening.

2. Look for examples of the background conversations taking place during meetings. How are they shaping the results?

3. To what extent do you see any of the characteristics of dialogue occurring in your organization? What would be the results of a dialogue process?

4. What type of conversations are taking place in your workplace? Are the various types of conversation taking place at the appropriate times?

Chapter 10

Achieving Breakthrough in Organizations

A Journey Of Discovery

"Once you have taken the impossible into your calculations, the possibilities become limitless."—Anonymous

Putting it all Together

In previous chapters I've created some unusual images of organizations to help you explore the dynamics that affect a company's success or failure. I've posed many questions to stretch your thinking about creating breakthrough. I don't claim to have a model that will solve the world's problems but I do have one that contains some very powerful possibilities. Organizations are unique and their inner workings are very complex. So this is not something that you can plug in and let it run. It requires careful thinking about the application of processes and techniques and it may require some outside consulting to give it that third-party perspective. These processes can bring tremendous excitement and fun into your work- place. People are born with a strong desire to succeed in their personal and organizational lives and want to be part of a winning team. They also are turned on by the knowledge that they are playing a key role in turning an organization into a winner.

A Journey of Discovery

I've called this process a journey of discovery for some important reasons. A journey signifies to me that we are covering some new, unexplored territory and that we are headed for an end point we haven't yet seen. A journey is usually undertaken with high interest, excitement, and commitment. A journey begins with an open mind, and a readiness for discovery. These all describe the breakthrough process we are about to begin. Some of you may remember the story of the *Abilene Paradox* by Jerry Harvey. A family was sitting around on a hot, boring afternoon wondering how they might entertain themselves when the grandfather suggested they drive to Abilene for dinner. Nobody wanted to do this (including the grandfather) but, since they all said OK (at least no one objected), they started off for the 2-hour drive. Only after they arrived did the fact come out that *none* of them had wanted to go in the first place. Many of the things we engage in within our organizations follow the same pattern. Think about all the things you are doing just because you assume that's the way it must be. If a journey of discovery follows this pattern, it will be a journey to nowhere.

In this journey we'll pass through a few provinces, each of which will make our job easier and increase our impetus. These provinces have overlapping borders and it won't always be clear when we are passing from one into another. The provinces are:

1. Environment for Breakthrough
2. Future Pull
3. Alignment
4. Empowerment
5. Creative Capacity
6. Just Do It

Environment for Breakthrough

It takes energy to create breakthrough and the first step is to create that energy if it doesn't already exist. An organization which is characterized by low morale and low energy needs something to get it started. I've used the term "defibrillation" to describe in a visual way what is necessary in some organizations. Let's hope your organization is not that ill.

Excitement must be injected into the group to get it thinking more positively about the future. It's a good time to concentrate on switching from a reactive to a creative orientation. You may want to review the definition of the Whack-A-Mole theory and the discussion of creative and reactive orientations in Chapter 1. Begin discussions that key in on what you want to create. Become sensitive to "mole-whacking." Encourage dialogue around the opportunities of a strong, positive future. Dialogue groups may engage in book reviews using several key books that help raise the level of thinking. Recommended books include this one (of course), *The Fifth Discipline, The Path of Least Resistance, Breakpoint and Beyond, Leadership and the New Science*, and C.K. Prahalad's *Strategic Intent* series in *Harvard Business Review*. See the book list in the appendix for further information about these, and other, books. It's important to build trust within the organization, particularly as it relates to the breakthrough and transformation. Many organizations have eroded their internal trust through past promises of change that never took place. If the trust level is low, there may be some front-end work needed to get it to the right level. Strong leaders create trust, and dialogue helps build it.

The environment for breakthrough and transformation has some guidelines that differ from those a normal organization may be used to. Here are a few of these guidelines:

- There are no mistakes. Failure is another word for learning. If we aren't failing much on our way to success then we probably aren't doing anything exciting. Create opportunities to reward some great "failures."

- Everyone should have an *in*, an *out*, and a *shake it all about* basket. Schedule ideation sessions often just to shake new ideas about and look for new possibilities. Promote spontaneous conversations for possibility and opportunity.
- Listen to others and always remember the value of diversity in thinking. Make a point to create diversity in all thinking activities. Strive to stamp out "Not Invented Here."
- Watch carefully for "Yeah-buts," your own and others, and always look for the gold in anything that's said. Try to create an environment in which individuals are always trying to add value to each others'thoughts.
- Seek opportunities to get out of your thinking box and off the beaten path. Be someone (or something) else, do something else, or think something else whenever you have an opportunity.
- Cast aside rational thinking and spend time asking "What if...?"
- Have frequent conversations for opportunity and possibility with others and look for opportunities for dialogue.
- Spend less time judging ideas (including your own) and more time asking what is good about them and what you can add.
- Don't take things too seriously. Lighten up and learn to enjoy your work. Learn to value the humor of your associates as a tremendous resource.

Future Pull

Volumes have been written about the visioning process and countless hours have been spent in corporate meeting rooms creating beautifully worded vision and mission statements to hang in reception areas and board rooms. I'm not talking about creating this kind of statement of vision. You need to plant a picture of what the company or group is capable of becoming in the minds of all associates. This must be a positive image of the future, one that is exciting and challenging, yet attainable. And it must include them in the picture. I don't know about you, but I'm not that interested in putting lots of energy into a future that doesn't include me.

This is where declarations become very important. The declaration of what is going to take place is a very strong source of future pull. Visions are pretty soft most of the time. Declarations are statements of fact. When the declaration is made, the future is created. Of course, the right person must make this declaration. For a declaration to create future pull it also must create a specific stretch event. If JFK had said, "I think we'll fly real high pretty soon," what would that have happened?

The following is a story told by John F. Kennedy. It shows the power of vision:

> Frank O'Conner, the Irish writer, tells in one of his books how, as a boy, he and his friends would make their way across the countryside and when they came to an orchard wall that seemed too high and too doubtful to try and too difficult to permit their voyage to continue, they took off their hats and tossed them over the wall — and then they had no choice but to follow them.

Another example of the power of vision comes from a story in a recent newspaper about Les Paul, the famous guitarist.

> It's hard to believe that Paul has acute arthritis that has immobilized all the fingers on his right hand and crippled all but two fingers on his left, or fingerboard hand. "I had to learn to play the guitar all over again as

the arthritis got worse," Paul says. "I play real good now with just two fingers." Paul also suffers from the effects of a 1948 automobile accident where he suffered a broken back, fractured pelvis, broken collarbone, broken ribs, a ruptured spleen and a right arm that was so crushed there was talk of amputating it.

Doctors managed to reconstruct the arm and set it pointed at Paul's navel in a guitar playing position. "It won't move but I can still hold a guitar," Paul says with a laugh. He has also been through bone graft surgery on his left hand; he has suffered from sciatica and Meniere's disease; he has had three operations on his right ear to correct a broken ear drum; and, in 1980, he underwent a quintuple heart-bypass operation at the Cleveland Clinic. "With every setback, every hospitalization, I've done some creating," he says. "If you can't play, you can think, you can sit there and invent." "So when someone says to me, 'You've had a lot of hardships'," I say, "But a lot of good things have come from them."

Wouldn't you like to have someone with that sort of drive on your team? If you can create a culture that successfully creates strong visions and future pull, it is possible to have people with the drive of Les Paul.

Alignment

When I see this word I think of my car's front end. When your car wheels are out of line they are going in different directions and it's easy to imagine the result on your driving. If people on a team are all going in different directions, it's easy to see the result on the overall effectiveness of the team. It makes no sense to empower without alignment. You'll simply wear down the people just like you'll wear out the tires on your misaligned car.

How do you achieve people alignment? Strong vision sure helps. Having healthy team dynamics also plays a major role. If there are significant problems with the relationships between people, there is some work to be done and I'd suggest you spend some time doing team building. Alignment also depends on how well the goals of the work relate to each individual's personal goals. People need to know they are making a valuable contribution to their world.

Empowerment

Giving individuals more personal power to use their abilities is important. Remember, empowerment in an unaligned situation creates internal conflict. So make sure there is alignment before empowerment. In an organization you can empower both thinking and action. You can create opportunities for individuals to *think* at a higher level and you can create opportunities to let them *do* more on their own. The best way to empower *thinking* is to allow an unbridled process of inquiry into the patterns or paradigms that, if shifted, can help create real transformative change. The best way to empower *doing* is to get out of the way.

Creative Potential

As discussed in Chapter 7 there is a tremendous amount of unused creative capacity in organizations. Now that you've created an environment for breakthrough, have a strong vision for future pull, have associates that are aligned in their energy, and have empowered both thinking and action, you are ready to unleash this creativity.

Creative thinking can be taught. I've taught hundreds of people how to enhance their creative skills and many have told me that it changed their lives forever. Creative thinking skills open opportunities for people and transform them into "kids in a candy store." It can bring back the excitement in work and can add tremendous potential to the energy and driving forces of teams. It can change the conversations in the workplace from whining about the past and transform them to real dialogue about the future. Creative processes can begin an upward spiral toward the development of things you never thought possible.

So, how do you go about developing the creativity in your organization? It's probably best to seek an outside consultant with the necessary skills who can help you with this training or help to develop your internal consultants. It's a very specialized field, and most companies have not developed that skill within their own staffs. There are growing numbers of specialists in creativity and several organizations and networks devoted to creating forums in this area.

Just Do it

Steal a page from Nike. At some point you need to stop messing around and just go for it. Creating a great future begins when you start to move in roughly the right direction. It never happens while you're standing still. American Indian stories and myths are wonderful learning tools for guiding change. I'll leave you with this one.

Many years ago, a young man and his grandfather spent their days together, as was the custom. The old man spent much time teaching the boy how to hunt, fish, and make things, and to do it all in a sacred way. Having lived many years, the grandfather possessed many great powers of healing and teaching. Great was his knowledge of many things. One day the grandfather said to the boy, "We will change the course of the mighty river."

The boy was filled with wonder, for he knew that his grandfather was a great man and could do great things. But change the course of a great river? Who of mortal man could accomplish such a great deed?

As they approached the river, the boy's heart leapt as he imagined the course of the river being changed. When they got to the bank of the river, the old man reached down into the river and picked out a rock about the size of a melon.

The boy watched as the hole that the rock left began to fill with water, and he understood that in some small way the old man had indeed changed the course of the mighty river.

The old man looked at the boy with a twinkle in his eye and said, "This is the way the great river is changed. One rock at a time. It is the duty of every man who walks to change the course of rivers. Every action that you do, every word that you say will affect or change the course of a person's life. Keep on changing the course of rivers, little one." Grandfather was a wise man.

Appendix 1 - Suggested Readings

Autry, James A., Love & Profit, William Morrow and Company, New York, 1991

Barker, Joel, Discovering the Future; The Business of Paradigms, (video), Charthouse Learning International, St. Paul, 1987

Barry, David, Claw Your Way to the Top, Rodale Press, Emmaus, PA., 1986

Bennis, Warren, Leaders, Harper and Row, New York, 1985

Cousins, Norman, Anatomy of an Illness, Bantam Books, New York, 1979

Covey, Stephen, The 7 Habits of Highly Effective People, Simon and Schuster, New York, 1991

Edwards, Betty, Drawing on the Right Side of the Brain, J.P. Tarcher, Inc., Los Angeles, 1979

Fritz, Robert, The Path of Least Resistance, Fawcett Columbine, New York, 1989

Gallway, Timothy, The Inner Game of Tennis, Bantam Books, New York, 1974

Harvey, Jerry, The Abilene Paradox, Lexington Books, Lexington, 1988

Hawken, Paul, Growing a Business, Simon and Schuster, New York, 1987

Kriegel, Robert, If It Ain't Broke - Break It, Warner Books, New York, 1991

Kuhn, Thomas, The Structure of Scientific Revolutions, University of Chicago Press, 1962

Land, George, Grow or Die, John Wiley & Sons, New York, 1986

Land, George, Breakpoint and Beyond, Harper Business, New York, 1992

Prahalad, C.K., Strategic Intent, Harvard Business Review, May-June 1989

Ray, Michael, Creativity in Business, Doubleday & Company, New York, 1986

Senge, Peter, The Fifth Discipline, Doubleday Currency, New York, 1990

Thomas, Warren D., Dolphin Conferences, Elephant Midwives, and Other Astonishing Facts About Animals, Jeremy Tarcher, Inc., Los Angeles, 1990

Van Gundy, Arthur B., Managing Group Creativity, AMACOM, 1984

Weller, Tom, The Book of Stupid Questions, Warner Books, New York, 1988

Wheatley, Margaret, Leadership and the New Science, Berrett-Koehler Publishers, San Francisco, 1992

BOOK ORDER FORM

Information: Date _____

Name: _____

Address:_____

City/State/Zip: _____

Phone/Fax: _____

__ Copies of the *Whack-A-Mole Theory* @ $12.95

__ Copies of *Get Out of Your Thinking Box* @ $7.95

Shipping is free to US - Please add $3 for Canada. New York residents please add 8% sales tax.

Both books make great handouts for group meetings. Generous quantity discounts are available. Call 716-334-4779 for information.

Make check payable to Creative Edge Associates and send to: PO Box 352, West Henrietta, NY 14586. We can also be reached via fax at 716-359-9744 or you may E-Mail Lindsay directly at LindsayCollier@msn.com.

An enticing family of workshops and presentations are available that are fun, fast moving, and powerful. Please call for information or check here if you'd like information on these sent to you. ____

BOOK ORDER FORM

Information: Date _____

Name: _____

Address:_____

City/State/Zip: _____

Phone/Fax: _____

__ Copies of the *Whack-A-Mole Theory* @ $12.95

__ Copies of *Get Out of Your Thinking Box* @ $7.95

Shipping is free to US - Please add $3 for Canada. New York residents please add 8% sales tax.

Both books make great handouts for group meetings. Generous quantity discounts are available. Call 716-334-4779 for information.

Make check payable to Creative Edge Associates and send to: PO Box 352, West Henrietta, NY 14586. We can also be reached via fax at 716-359-9744 or you may E-Mail Lindsay directly at LindsayCollier@msn.com.

An enticing family of workshops and presentations are available that are fun, fast moving, and powerful. Please call for information or check here if you'd like information on these sent to you. ____